T0295729

Social Capital's Impact on Innovation: Bright Side, Dark Side or Both?

Wang Zhan

 Paths International Ltd

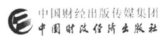 中国财经出版传媒集团
中国财政经济出版社

I dedicate this book to the memory of

my beloved grandmother.

Abstract

Various conceptual and empirical studies demonstrate that social capital is a powerful factor in fostering innovation. However, most research focuses solely on the benefits of social capital without considering potential downsides. Further research is needed to consider potential risks or negative consequences of social capital to develop a more objective understanding of social capital's potential negative outcomes. Moreover, social capital studies tend to examine social capital at only a single level, such as at the individual-level or firm-level, neglecting the effects operating simultaneously at both levels.

This research develops a multilevel model to hypothesize social decision-making constraints as the mediator between social capital and firm innovation. Furthermore, this study also considers culture as a moderator that exerts moderating effects on the relationship between social capital and social decision-making constraints. Social capital and social decision-making constraints, as well as culture are conceptualized as operating at both the individual-level and the firm-level, while innovation operates solely at the level of the firm.

A survey is used to collect multilevel data from individuals and firm managers. Survey items from prior studies are adapted for this research. The sample is comprised of 1,007 employees working at 102 high-tech firms in China's Tianjin Economic-Technological Development Area (TEDA). Multilevel structural equation modelling (MSEM) is used to analyse the data. The results confirm the negative mediating role of social decision-making constraints, revealing that social capital influences social decision-making constraints at both the individual-level and firm-level, which in turn, impedes firm-level innovation.

When compared to previous studies, the findings offer a more comprehensive and precise understanding of the multilevel impacts of social capital on firm innovation by providing evidence of the negative mediating role of social decision-making constraints. In contrast to the dominant view in the literature that social capital is always a positive phenomenon, social capital can potentially harm firm innovation performance. From the managerial perspective, the supported hypotheses suggest that social capital is a precondition for innovation, but a clear understanding of the costs and potential risks of investing in social capital needs to be weighed carefully against its potential benefits.

Table of Contents

List of Tables

v

List of Figures

List of Abbreviations

ANOVA	Analysis of Variance
CFI	Comparative Fit Index
CFA	Confirmatory Factor Analysis
EFA	Exploratory Factor Analysis
FDI	Foreign Direct Investment
ICC	Intra-class Correlation
MCFA	Multilevel Confirmatory Factor Analysis
ML	Maximum Likelihood
MLM	Multilevel Modelling
MSEM	Multilevel Structural Equation Modelling
NACE	nomenclature statistique des activités économiques dans la Communauté européenne
OECD	Organizational for Economic Co-operation and Development
R&D	Research and Development
RMSEA	Root Mean Square Error of Approximation
SEM	Structural Equation Modelling
SPSS	Statistical Product and Service Solutions
SRMR	Standardized Root Mean Square Residual
TBNA	Tianjin Binhai New Area
TEDA	Tianjin Economic-Technological Development Area
TLI	Tucker-Lewis Index
WTO	World Trade Organization

Chapter 1

Introduction

1. 1   Introduction

This opening chapter presents an overview of the study in order to contextualise the subsequent chapters. Firstly, the introduction outlines the background and rationale for this study, highlighting the central constructs which drive the study. Following this, the research questions which are derived from the gaps identified in the existing literature are presented. Specifically, this chapter aims to provide a justification for this study, as well as to outline the research objectives and contributions. The remainder of this chapter is structured as follows: Section 1. 2 details the research background and rationale. Section 1. 3 provides definitions of key constructs. Section 1. 4 outlines the research questions and research objectives. Section 1. 5 highlights the research contributions. Section 1. 6 provides details concerning the book structure. Section 1. 7 provides a conclusion to this introductory chapter.

1. 2   Research background and rationale

In knowledge-based economies, innovation is believed to be an important determining factor in the development, growth and survival of firms (Vander Panne et al. 2003; Pervan et al. 2009; Varis and Littunen 2010; Yu 2013) . Innovation is not a new phenomenon, dating back to the seminal works of Schumpeter (1934; 1939). Since the 1980s, interest in innovation has grown in the management and economic literatures. This initial interest was fuelled by the fast-growing and dynamic nature of high technology industries such as telecommunication and computer programming (Balogun et al. 2008), which rely on constant innovation. Over time, innovation has become as much a managerial issue as a technological one (Elke U. Weber et al. 2005). Moreover, due to the dynamic, emergent and unpredictable nature of the innovation process, the study of innovation remains a challenge for academics and practitioners alike (McKelvey et al. 2015; Ou et al. 2016).

Firm-level innovation refers to the implementation of new products (or services), processes, marketing and organizational methods in a firm. However, possessing numerous creative ideas does not necessarily translate into highly innovative performance (Li et al. 2013). Therefore, it is necessary to identify the factors that restrict the application of a creative idea, which can result in hampering innovation performance (Hmieleski and Baron 2009; Wu and Chaturvedi 2009).

Furthermore, innovation is created primarily by investment in intangibles (Subramaniam and Youndt 2005). Social capital is generally defined as the sum of resources that are embedded in social relationships, which is much less tangible that other capital, such as human capital and financial capital (Coleman 1990; Nahapiet and Ghoshal 1998). Social capital, therefore, has received much attention as a determinant of innovation in recent years (Landry et al. 2002; Subramaniam and Youndt 2005; Zheng 2010; Fulmer and Gelfand 2012). This is primarily driven by knowledge being considered as the solid foundation of innovation in the era of the knowledge economy, reflecting the main driving force of competitive advantage (Filieri et al. 2014). Hence, it is imperative to access and exploit knowledge to generate innovation. Therefore, given that knowledge sharing has been widely regarded by several scholars to be one of the major and direct benefits of social capital (e. g. Nahapiet and Ghoshal 1998; Adler and Kwon 2002; Reagans and McEvily 2003; McFadyen and Cannella 2004; Inkpen and Tsang 2005; Chiu et al. 2011), social capital is a powerful theory used to explain how to access knowledge through relationships that can influence innovation outputs (Filieri et al. 2014).

Various conceptual and empirical studies have demonstrated that social capital is a powerful factor in terms of fostering innovation through accessing, transferring and sharing knowledge (e. g. Nahapiet and Ghoshal 1998; Adler and Kwon 2002; Wu 2008). However, given that both individuals and firms invest significant resources to build social capital within their network, further research needs to consider the potential risks or negative consequences associated with social capital (Villena et al. 2011). Indeed, social capital can give rise to appropriable resources for use, yet it is also important to acknowledge the fact that such social capital can also lead to potentially negative outcomes, such as opportunistic behaviour, unproductive reciprocation and decision-making constraints, which, in turn, may harm innovation performance (McFadyen and Cannella 2004; Villena et al. 2011; Li et al. 2013; Zhou et al. 2014).

The rationale for this study emerges from the fact that a very limited number of studies on the social capital-innovation relationship have addressed the negative effects of social capital on innovation. Although some studies have explored and highlighted the presence of the negative outcomes of social capital (e. g. Portes 1998; Adler and Kwon 2002), few studies have empirically confirmed the negative consequences of social capital (Li et al. 2013). Investigating the potentially negative consequences associated with social capital has important managerial implications, given that indiscriminate promotion of social capital may lead to a waste of resources (Portes 1998), and blindly calling for the building of higher levels of social capital can harm rather than enhance innovation performance (Villena et al. 2011). Therefore, in addition to emphasizing the benefits of social capital, a good understanding of the negative consequences associated with social capital can facilitate a more objective evaluation of investment in social capital.

This study fills the gap in the prevailing literature by highlighting the negative aspects of social capital. Social decision-making constraints, which refer to the factors introduced by a social relationship that can control decision-making, is identified here as one of the specific negative consequences of social capital. This merits investigation, as social decision-making constraints have significant effects on innovation performance (Li et al. 2013). The autonomy of individuals is likely to be reduced when individuals derive benefits by accessing and sharing knowledge through their social capital, given that social norms and controls may constrain individuals by sacrificing the freedom to make decisions, to a certain extent. Consequently, possessing numerous creative ideas does not necessarily translate into highly innovative performance. Due to network solidarity, it is necessary to consider other network members' views in order to decide whether or not to implement an innovative idea. This is an expression of the age-old dilemma between individual freedom and network solidarity (Portes 1998). Accordingly, the identification of social decision-making constraints as a specific negative outcome associated with social capital is indispensable for evaluating investment in social capital more objectively and understanding the identification of social decision-making constraints as an innovation barrier that can enable individuals and firms to overcome it. Therefore, this study aims to examine how social capital influences the firm's innovation performance via the effects of social decision-making constraints.

In addition to the above, most management issues in a firm, including the firm's innovation, involve multilevel phenomena (Brass et al. 2004; Hitt et al. 2007). Specifically, innovation is at least a two-level phenomenon, and involves both an actor (e. g. an individual) and the broader environment (e. g. a firm) in which the actor is embedded (Eveleens 2017). Along with this, in order to offer a comprehensive understanding of innovation, it is necessary to understand how constructs at one level influence innovation at another level. However, most social capital-innovation studies have been largely limited to a single level, with both dependent variables (i. e. innovation) and independent variables (i. e. social capital) conceptualized and measured at the same level (Ibarra et al. 2005; Payne et al. 2011). That is to say, most prior social capital studies have explored how social capital within the networks of individuals, groups or firms relates to innovation at the same level of analysis, neglecting the multilevel phenomena of innovation with the nesting nature of individuals within a firm. Although some previous studies have already addressed the nested nature of individual networks in groups, few empirical works have employed a multilevel methodology to examine the cross-level bridges between variables at different levels of analysis (Moliterno and Mahony 2011). As an example, it is necessary to investigate how the behaviours and perceptions of different individuals together impact a firm's innovation performance.

Therefore, when examining how social capital influences firm-level innovation, it is critical to identify the appropriate levels at which social capital operates. Social capital can be obtained at different levels (Zheng 2010). As it involves the collection of resources, social capital resides in both two individuals' relationships and the whole collective into which individuals form (Nahapiet and Ghoshal 1998; Tsai and Ghoshal 1998; Yu et al. 2013). Accordingly, considering the nested nature of firms in which employees are situated, it is the worthwhile aim of this study to adopt a multilevel approach to examine the effects of social capital at both individual-level and firm-level. An individual's social interactions help to establish the firm-level social capital, which, in turn, influences firm-level innovation performance (Bizzi 2013; Yu et al. 2013). Hence, it is necessary to conceptually distinguish social capital at firm-level from that of social capital at the individual-level. This is particularly important for demonstrating the multilevel effects of social capital on a firm's innovation performance.

Moreover, given that culture can motivate individuals' behaviours, it is essential to avoid neglecting cultural influences in social capital studies (Webster and White 2010; Kemper et al. 2011). However, few studies of social capital have considered cultural issues to date. Rather than adopt country-level categorisation in terms of cultural values directly, one would anticipate significant differences in individuals' responses to such cultural values within a country (McSweeney 2002). Considering that social capital is explored at the levels of individuals and firms, this study addresses pertinent cultural factors at individual-level (i. e. an individual's perceptions) and firm-level (i. e. all employees' perceptions) in order to examine the moderating effects on the context in which the negative outcome of social capital occurs.

In summary therefore, the prime aim of this study is to examine the mediating role of social decision-making constraints in reducing the positive effect of individual social capital on a firm's innovation performance, in addition to the moderating impact of culture on the relationship between social capital and social decision-making constraints. China serves as the locale for the current research. Thus, the question arises: what makes China a suitable and interesting research context? The next section provides an explanation.

China's Tianjin Economic-technological Development Area (TEDA)

The China National Economic-technological Development Areas are not only special areas in China where foreign direct investment (FDI) occurs, but are also the areas in which the local high-technology industry can expand. TEDA is one of China's earliest development areas, and has ranked first in the General Evaluation on National Level Development Area for 17 successive years (Magni et al. 2017). The reasons that China's TEDA serves as an interesting research context are as follows:

Social capital theories have been well-supported in most research based on Western countries. It is worth noting that most of the studies have collected data from Western countries, such as the United States and the United Kingdom. This seems to reflect the view that the concept of social capital is much less commonly adopted in China. However, China is well-known to be a relationship-rich society (Kogut and Zander 1992; Wu 2008), which can provide a supportive context for testing the issues related to social capital, contributing significantly to the understanding of social capital theory. As most of the studies have been extensively undertaken in Western countries, the outcome is limited in terms of generalizability. Therefore, the results from indigenous firms in non-Western contexts can help to test the generalizability of the existing social capital theories, which are largely Western in origin (Wu 2008). Conducting the study in China is more likely to generate meaningful and lasting implications for academia and practitioners.

This study aims to examine the moderating effects of culture at both individual and firm level. After joining the World Trade Organization (WTO), the cultural values in China are increasingly diverse, ranging from traditional Chinese cultural values to international cultural influences from developed economies (Schyns and Sanders 2006; Liden 2012). This diversity in cultural values provides a suitable context in which to test the within-country variance of culture.

This research selects high-technology firms as the target firms, given that high-technology firms are characterized by constant innovation, providing a proper setting for testing the relationship between social capital and innovation (Batjargal 2003b; Uhl-Bien and Maslyn 2003; Taras et al. 2010). TEDA serves as a place where 234 Chinese local high-technology firms and 3,734 scientific and technological small and medium firms are located. Drawing a sample from these firms thus ensures a reasonable sample size.

Considering the advantages listed above, all indicate that China's TEDA serves as an interesting and suitable research context when examining the effects of social capital on innovation.

Having examined the background and rationale for this study, the overall aim of this study is to explore the relationship between social capital at both individual and firm level, and innovation performance at the firm level, highlighting the mediating effects of social decision-making constraints and the moderating effects of culture. Therefore, it is essential to address the key concepts in the study to provide a background to the subsequent research. Definitions of innovation, social capital, social decision-making constraints and culture are presented in the next section.

1.3   Definition of key concepts

Before presenting the research questions, it is essential to define the key concepts in this study, in order to provide a background to the subsequent research analysis. Table 1.1 outlines the key constructs and their relevant research level.

Table 1.1   Key constructs and research level

Key construct	Level of research
Innovation	Firm-level
Social capital	Individual- and firm-level
Social decision making constraints	Individual- and firm-level
Culture	Individual- and firm-level

For the purpose of this study, innovation refers to the implementation of new products (or services), processes, marketing and organizational methods in a firm. The above definition of innovation, and a more detailed discussion on the different roles of innovation as a process or as an outcome, is presented in Section 2. 3.

Furthermore, as an important determinant of innovation, this study defines social capital at both levels of individual and firm. At the individual-level, social capital is defined as resources embedded in individuals' relationships that are available to exchange through the relationships. Considering the nested nature of individuals in firms, firm-level social capital is based on the aggregation of individual-level social capital, referring to the aggregation of resources embedded in the relationships among members of a firm. A further discussion on the definition and conceptualization of social capital as adopted by Nahapiet and Ghoshal's framework (1998) is provided in Section 2. 4.

While social capital makes resources exchangeable through relationships, it also imposes constraints on the decision-making for those who use these resources. Considering the parallel connection with social capital at both individual- and firm-level, the construct of social decision-making constraints is in need of definition at both levels. At the individual-level, the construct of social decision-making constraints refer to the individual's perception regarding the extent to which factors introduced by social relationships can control his/her decision-making in undertaking a task. At the firm-level, social decision-making constraints refer to the aggregated perception of involved individuals within the firm regarding the extent to which factors introduced by social relationships can control their decision-making in undertaking a task. A more detailed discussion of the definition, as well as the two main determinants of social decision-making constraints, in terms of network conformity and hierarchical structure, is presented in Section 2. 5.

The aim of this study is to investigate the moderating effects of culture on social capital and social decision-making constraints at both individual- and firm-level. Thus, for the purpose of this study, individual-level culture is defined as individuals' beliefs, values, attitudes and norms that distinguish one group of individuals from another by influencing their behaviours. The firm-level culture aggregates the individuals' perception, referring to aggregated beliefs, values, attitudes and norms of involved individuals within a firm. In addition, Section 2. 6 presents two specific dimensions of culture, and justifies the relevance of these two specific dimensions to examine the relationship between social capital and social decision-making constraints.

7

Following from the above definitions of key constructs in this research, the related research questions and objectives are outlined in the next section.

1.4 Research questions and objectives

The aim of this section is to outline the research questions and related objectives. By analysing empirical data for high-tech firms in China, this study addresses the research questions that inform the research objective. The main research question for this study can be stated as follows:

What is the mediating role of social decision-making constraints in the relationships between individual- and firm-level social capital and firm-level innovation performance?

This research question gives rise to the following key research objective:

To develop a comprehensive multilevel model that investigates the relationships between social capital and innovation through social decision-making constraints.

Arising from this main objective, two specific research questions emerge, as follows:

1. At the individual-level, what are the relationships between social capital and social decision-making constraints?

2. At the firm-level, how does social decision-making constraints mediate the relationships between social capital and innovation performance?

Resulting from the questions above, a further question emerges regarding the perspective of culture:

How does culture influence the relationships between social capital and social decision-making constraints at both individual- and firm-level?

From this, the second objective is identified as follows:

To determine whether, and to what extent, culture influences the effects of social capital on social decision-making constraints at both the individual- and the firm-level.

Having presented the rationale, research questions and objectives, the next section outlines the major contributions of this study.

1.5 Research contributions

Using China as the research context, this study adopts a multilevel approach to investigate the relationship between individual- and firm-level social capital and firm-level innovation through the route of social decision-making constraints, with an emphasis on cultural factors. More specifically, in addressing the research questions and objectives outlined in Section 1.4, this study makes the following original and timely contributions:

1.5.1   Theoretical contributions

This study enriches social capital theory by shedding light on its negative consequences in terms of social decision-making constraints. Previous research has largely focused on the benefits of social capital, whereas, its negative effects have received limited attention. This study advances the understanding of multilevel phenomena in social capital-innovation studies by considering the nesting nature of individuals within the firm, providing a comprehensive understanding of how a firm's innovation performance can be influenced by social capital.

Given that no conceptual model of the social capital-innovation relationship in the existing literature has included cultural factors, this research fills this gap by developing a comprehensive model to illustrate how social capital negatively influences innovation with the consideration of cultural influences. This research focuses on the within-country variance of cultural value in China, extending previous findings that assume homogeneity among all individuals in a society by considering culture at both levels of the individual and the firm.

1.5.2   Empirical contributions

To test the proposed model of the social capital-innovation relationship, survey data were collected from a large field sample of employees nested within firms (1,007 employees in 102 firms). This study uses a relatively novel analysis approach in terms of multilevel structural equation modelling, given that it can appropriately account for the hierarchical data structure that causes dependencies in the data.

On the grounds that existing literature has been largely developed in Western countries, this research is unique in developing and implementing a survey in the Chinese context. The methodological approach applied and analysed in China has the potential to test the generalizability of the existing Western-based theories.

1. 5. 3   Managerial contributions

This study provides a clear understanding that the costs and potential risks of investing in social capital need to be weighed carefully against its potential benefits.

Since 2010, China has emerged as the world's second largest economy, and the largest exporter and manufacturer (Lai and Gibbons 1997). Considering the importance of Chinese firms in global business, this research provides some valuable insights into the current social capital and innovation activities of Chinese firms. The research findings could be used not only by Chinese firms, but also by Western firms, to better understand Chinese firms.

Based on the above discussion, the next section provides a synopsis of the structure of the book.

1. 6   Structure of the book

To address the research aims and questions, the subsequent chapters of the book are following. Chapter 2 presents a critical literature review in the area of innovation, social capital, social decision-making constraints and culture. Chapter 3 addresses previous studies of the social capital-innovation relationship constructed by other researchers, and develops a comprehensive empirical model and hypotheses to be tested for investigating the interrelationships among the four constructs reviewed in Chapter 2. Chapter 4 discusses the methodological approaches to be followed in the research, highlighting the research design and field design, as well as the development of survey items. Chapter 5 details the complete process of data verification and analysis, as well as presenting the results of the analysis. Chapter 6 concludes this study by explaining and interpreting the results with the support of literature, and concludes with theoretical and managerial implications emanating from the study's findings. Chapter 7 concludes the book, indicating the contributions and limitations of the research, as well as suggesting some directions for future research.

1. 7   Conclusion

The dearth of research relating to the negative effects of social capital on innovation has been highlighted through a review of social capital theory. The main aim of this study, therefore, is to address this gap by developing a comprehensive

model, which combines innovation, social capital, social decision-making constraints, and cultural factors. Through the development of a conceptual model of
the social capital-innovation relationship (by considering the negative outcomes of
social capital and cultural influences), this book contributes to the social capital
literature by shedding light on its negative consequences, as well as providing insights into the moderating effects of culture. The relevant literature is reviewed in
the next chapter, which serves to contextualize the research undertaken in this
study.

Chapter 2

Literature Review

2. 1   Introduction

Social capital has received much attention as a determinant of innovation in recent years (Landry et al. 2002). However, in spite of the vast number of studies on social capital-innovation relationships, there is still a lacuna of theoretical and empirical research confirming the effects of the negative consequences of social capital on innovation, as extant studies focus primarily on the positive effects of social capital (Lechner et al. 2010; Villena et al. 2011; Li et al. 2013). Moreover, culture is an influential construct which can strengthen social capital's outcome, yet this link has also been under-researched in the literature (Kemper et al. 2011). This book, therefore, contributes to the study of the relationship between social capital and innovation by considering the mediating effects of the negative outcomes of social capital, in terms of social decision-making constraints. Additionally, this study takes specific cultural dimensions into account, which can moderate the relationship between social capital and social decision-making constraints.

In the context of the above, in order to establish a theoretical foundation for the arguments presented in this study, it is helpful to review the key literature streams. To that end, this chapter focuses on reviewing and integrating the literature in the areas of innovation, social capital and its negative effect in terms of social decision-making constraints, as well as culture. Before reviewing the literature on these constructs, Section 2. 2 provides a specific discussion on the research level of each construct, namely, that innovation is conceptualized and operated at the firm-level, social capital and culture are defined and conceptualized at the individual-level, and then aggregated into firm-level as contextual effects. Therefore, the conceptualization and definition of firm-level innovation are discussed in Section 2. 3. Section 2. 4 presents a review of definitions and conceptualizations of social capital at both the individual- and firm-level by adopting Nahapiet and Ghoshal's (1998) three dimensions in terms of structural, relational and cognitive social capital. The literature on social decision-making constraints, as a specific negative consequence of social capital in this study, is reviewed in Section 2. 5 by examining the definition and determinants. Section 2. 6 provides a discussion of the definition of culture and a theoretical explanation of two specific cultural dimensions. Section 2. 7 justifies why China is appropriate as the research context in this study. Section 2. 8 concludes the chapter.

2. 2　Research level of each construct

In an organization, most management issues, including firm-level innovation, involve multilevel phenomena (Brass et al. 2004; Hitt et al. 2007). According to Gupta et al. (2017), all innovation is at least a two-level phenomenon that involves an actor (e. g. an individual) and the broader environment in which the actor is embedded (e. g. a firm). However, most innovation studies have mainly focused on one level of analysis and it is rare to read about how constructs at one level influence innovation at another level. Additionally, when examining how social capital influences firm-level innovation, appropriate levels of social capital are critical. Therefore, given the complexities associated with different levels of analysis (Hitt et al. 2007), before reviewing the main constructs in this book, it is necessary to clarify the theoretical basis of multilevel issues.

The multilevel principle is concerned with how constructs are related across levels of analysis (Gupta et al. 2007). That organizational entities reside in nested arrangements is the central theme of multilevel constructs (Hitt et al. 2007). Many firm-level innovation phenomena originate in the form of individual behaviours and perceptions (Eveleens 2017). This is due to the fact that individuals are nested in firms, and each firm is composed of an intra-firm network of firm members (Moliterno and Mahony 2011). Every individual in the firm can be relatively independent of each other. Individuals' interactions mutually reinforce each other, and further influence the contextual environment of the firm (Perlow et al. 2004). In other words, actions and reactions among individuals give rise to collective phenomena, referred to as shared perception of "the events, practices and the kind of behaviours that get rewarded, supported, and expected in a setting" (Song 2009, p. 833). Furthermore, despite variations across individuals who hold their own perceptions, there tends to be a single perception that dominates within a firm. Therefore, the perception aggregated across involved individuals within a firm can represent the prevailing perception in the firm (Richardson and Smith 2007).

The question arises as to how individual perceptions combine within a firm to reflect the firm-level perception. Marsh et al. (2014) provide a conceptual framework to distinguish two different types of higher level constructs, in terms of climate and contextual effects, which are based on the aggregation of lower level constructs. Firstly, it is important to appropriately distinguish between climate and contextual effects.

Climate effects are those that originate from aggregations of individuals' evaluation of firm characteristics (Alexander and Van Knippenberg 2014). In this sense, the referent is the firm, in that individuals in the firm respond to some aspect of the firm. In other words, individuals are directly asked to evaluate their firm and are thus theoretically interchangeable. Climate effects therefore depict individuals' shared perceptions regarding their firm's environment (Song and Montoya-weiss 1998). Ideally, responses to climate constructs should be in agreement and tend to be correlated among individuals within the same firm.

By contrast, contextual effects are those of a firm construct above the effect of the corresponding individual-level construct. The referent is individuals and the firm-level construct is an aggregation of these different individuals' characteristics. The responses for contextual constructs are not expected to be correlated and interchangeable as random variation across individuals in the same firm is expected (Song and Montoya-weiss 1998; Sheremata 2004; Alexander and Van Knippenberg 2014).

Of direct relevance to this study, when considering the firm-level constructs that are aggregated from the individual-level, the effects of social capital and culture represent contextual effects. This is due to the fact that at the individual-level, social capital and culture represent the characteristic of each individual, not the firm. Firm-level social capital and culture are aggregated by individual characteristics that are specific to each individual in the firm. Here, the referent of the construct in terms of social capital and culture is the individual rather than the firm.

The above discussion makes it clear that the construct of social capital (including the specific negative consequence of social decision-making constraints) and culture should first and foremost be studied at the individual-level and properly represented as contextual effects at the firm-level.

Rousseau (1986) provides a useful framework to guide scholars simultaneously considering the levels of theory and levels of measurement. The level of theory represents the level at which the constructs are expected to operate or exist, whereas the level of measurement refers to the level at which the construct is measured (Gupta et al. 2007). In summary, regarding the level of theory in this study, the construct of innovation is solely conceptualized at firm-level, whereas constructs of social capital, social decision-making constraints and culture are conceptualized at the individual-level first, and then represented as contextual effects at the firm-level. Moreover, the level of measurement must be critically aligned with the level of theory. The level of theory provides justification for the level of measurement of each construct, which will be discussed in Chapter 4.

From Section 2. 3 to 2. 7, the literature on these constructs is specifically reviewed.

2. 3   Innovation

The word innovation was derived from the Latin verb "innovare" in the mid-1500s, meaning renew, alter or make new. Innovation has always been an essential driving factor for the development of society and organizations (Porter 1990; Lundvall 2010; Jimenez-Jimenez and Sanz-Valle 2011); however, it was not until the early twentieth century that it began to attract the attention of economists (Mowery and Rosenberg 1999).

Schumpeter (1934) who pinpoints the unique significance of innovation to business evolution, has been cited as the principal founder of innovation theory among the first group of economists. In his book, The Theory of Economic Development: An Inquiry into Profits, Capital, Credit, Interest and the Business Cycle, Schumpeter (1934) assumes that the source of economic growth is "creative destruction":

> "The fundamental impulse that sets and keeps the capitalist engine in motion comes from the new consumers' goods, the new methods of production or Transportation, the new markets...[This process] incessantly revolutionizes the economic structure within, incessantly destroying the old one, incessantly creating a new one. This process of Creative Destruction is the essential fact about capitalism. "
>
> (Schumpeter 1934, p. 83)

In contrast to neoclassical economics which indicates that the efficient allocation of scarce resources is the source of economic growth, Schumpeter's (1934) creative destruction theory argues that innovation is the key engine for growth. Further, his later work, Business Cycles, specifically suggests that innovative firms could change the economic equilibrium by making older products and processes obsolete, and thereby, create more value to ensure their success and survival in the long run (Schumpeter 1939). Schumpeter's theory of "creative destruction" has initiated a new understanding of innovation as a driving force in economic growth, which has become the central theme of modern innovation literature.

According to Schumpeter (1934, p. 66), innovation could involve one of the following scenarios:
- the introduction of a new good or of a new quality of a good;
- the introduction of a new method of production;
- the opening of a new market;
- the conquest of a new source of supply;
- the carrying out of the new organisation of an industry.

His view of innovation is primarily focused on manufacturing or the development of tangible goods, disregarding innovation in services (Goffin and Mitchell 2005; Lillis et al. 2015). One possible reason for this might be the business milieu of that time, namely that economies were greatly reliant on manufacturing. However, as the service sector has developed rapidly over the last few decades, innovation scholars have been urged to broaden aspects of innovation to reflect the requirement of the new business setting. Van de ven et al. (1999, p. 13) incorporate services by defining innovation as "the development and implementation of new ideas and knowledge into a socially and economically successful product, process or service".

2. 3. 1   Innovation as outcomes

Innovation as an outcome should answer the questions "what" or "what kind". The diverse classifications of innovation varying in magnitude, scope, and type deal specifically with these questions (Crossan and Apaydin 2010; Adamczyk et al. 2012).

The magnitude classification of innovation indicates the degree of newness of the innovation outcome (Gopalakrishnan and Damanpour 1997). In this context, two types of innovation can be identified as follows: radical innovation which concerns major departures from the firm's existing capabilities and constitute the basis for completely new products and services that are new to the world, and incremental innovation which represents minor changes and modifications to existing products, services, routines and operations (Garcia and Calantone 2002; Ritala and Hurmelinna-Laukkanen 2013; Menguc et al. 2014).

In terms of the scope of change, Gopalakrishnan and Damanpour (1997) indicate that innovation can be divided into two types: technological and administrative innovation. Technological innovation refers to the adoption of ideas that directly influence product/service and process. Conversely, administrative innovation involves changes that affect allocation of resources, policies, human resources and other factors that are more directly related with managerial aspects of organizations.

The most widespread classification of innovation can be characterized in terms of types. In this context, Schumpeter's (1934) seminal research identifies two fundamental types of this classification: product and process innovation. Further, the range of this classification has been broadened to cover marketing and organizational innovation, as well as incorporating services into product innovation (OECD[1] 2005). Compared to Schumpeter, who only differentiates between two types of innovation, the classification using the OECD methodology is more comprehensive and provides a wide range of possible innovation types.

Moreover, the scope and type of the classification are closely related: technological innovation is often associated with product and process innovation, while administrative innovation is more often associated with marketing and organizational innovation. However, the scope of the classification only relates to a more general distinction between the social structure and technical systems of an organization; by contrast, the OECD classification encompasses more specific innovation types which can be more easily measured. Table 2.1 summarises this classification in terms of product, process, marketing and organizational innovation in accordance with the OECD methodology.

Table 2.1   **Four types of innovation according to the OECD methodology**

Type of Innovation	Definition	Distinctive Characteristics
Product Innovation	The introduction of a good or service that is new or significantly improved with respect to its characteristics or intended uses	Significant changes in technical specifications, components and materials, incorporated software, user friendliness or other functional characteristics
Purpose: To develop functional characteristics of products or services		
Process Innovation	The implementation of a new or significantly improved method of production or delivery	Significant changes in techniques, equipment and/or software

---

[1]   Organization for Economic Co-operation and Development

continued

Type of Innovation	Definition	Distinctive Characteristics
Purpose: To reduce unit costs of production or delivery, to increase quality, or to produce or deliver new or significantly improved products		
Organizational Innovation	The implementation of a new organizational method	Significant improvements in the firm's business practices, workplace, organizations or external relations
Purpose: To reduce administrative costs or transaction costs, improve workplace satisfaction, gain access to non-tradable assets, or reduce cost of supplies		
Marketing Innovation	The implementation of a new marketing method involving significant changes	Significant changes in product design or packaging, product placement, product promotion or pricing
Purpose: To better address customers' needs, open up new markets, or newly position a firm's product on the market with the objective of increasing sales		

Source: OECD (2005, p. 48 −51)

The OECD classification was developed in the Oslo Manual in 2005. However, it has not become out-dated and remains the primary international source of guidelines for defining and classifying innovation (Kafetzopoulos and Psomas 2015). In line with the suggested innovation types, the OECD (2015) latest report "OECD Science, Technology and Industry Scoreboard 2015: Innovation for growth and society" adopts this classification to analyse percentages of each innovation type with different firm sizes and sectors in 37 countries. Regarding academic studies, multiple scholars have adopted this classification to conceptualise and measure innovation in their current research (e. g. Gunday et al. 2011; Wong 2013; Kafetzopoulos and Psomas 2015) .

In summary, in order to explain the view of innovation as an outcome, this section specifically reviews three classifications of innovation according to different magnitude, scope and type.

2. 3. 2 Defining firm-level innovation

Innovation is a broad and complex construct, with different researchers defining it from alternative perspectives with different emphases. With an emphasis on knowledge, innovation refers to new knowledge incorporated in products, processes and services (Afuah 1998), or "the commercial application of new knowledge" (Love et al. 2011, p. 1438). When defining the concept narrowly as technical innovation in hardware and software, innovation is the combination of technologies or a new technology that can provide benefits (McDermott and O Connor 2002). From an organizational or firm perspective, scholars who view innovation as a process, define innovation as the creation and implementation of new ideas (Carnabuci and Diószegi 2015); on the other hand, scholars who view innovation as an outcome, define innovation as "a new product, service, process, market, organizational structure, or administrative system" (Damanpour and Wischnevsky 2006, p. 271).

Before defining the construct of innovation, it is necessary to decide the emphasis of innovation in this study. The last two sections have focused on the different roles of innovation—as a process or as an outcome. The evolutionary innovation models explain the innovation process in Section 2.3.1, and three classifications of innovation explain the role of innovation as an outcome in Section 2.3.2. According to Crossan and Apaydin's (2010) study (which provides a systematic review of the literature on organization innovation published over 27 years), innovation as an outcome is usually the key dependent variable in empirical studies related to firm-level innovation. This is due to the fact that the role of innovation as an outcome is the result of a successful exploitation of an idea, which means it is both necessary and sufficient for a successful exploitation of an idea. On the other hand, innovation as a process is only the process of exploitation of an idea, which means it is necessary but not sufficient in itself. Therefore, the two roles of innovation are not equally important.

This study focuses on innovation as an outcome and views it as the dependent variable in the next chapter. Given this study's emphasis on innovation as an outcome, it is worth summarising how innovation is described as an outcome by Schumpeter, the founding father of innovation economics. According to Schumpeter (1934, p. 66), innovation involves the introduction of a new good, a new method of production, the opening of a new market, a new source of supply of raw materials and the carrying out of the new organization of an industry. This definition clearly specifies a wide range of possible innovation outcomes, but as alluded to earlier, this definition disregards innovation in services.

More recently, the OECD (2005), in its Oslo Manual, puts forward the following widely-accepted definition with the emphasis on innovation as an outcome.

> Innovation refers to "the implementation of a new or significantly improved product (good or service), or process, a new marketing method, or a new organizational method in business practices, workplace organization or external relationships. "
>
> OECD (2005, p. 46)

This definition views innovation as an outcome and leads to a distinction between four types of innovation: product, process, marketing and organizational innovation. Section 2. 3. 2 provides definitions corresponding to each type of innovation in line with the definition.

This study views innovation as the dependent variable by focusing on innovation as an outcome. This is due to the fact that innovation as an outcome is necessary and sufficient for the successful exploitation of an idea, whereas innovation as a process is only necessary but not sufficient in itself. Therefore, as an outcome of the successful acceptance and application of creative ideas, firm-level innovation refers to the implementation of new or significantly improved products (or services), processes, marketing and organizational methods in a firm.

Along with the definition, the classification of innovation according to four different types, in terms of product, process, marketing and organizational innovation has been adopted in this book.

Having established the relevant definitions related to innovation, and given that this book aims to examine how social capital negatively influences innovation, it is appropriate to review the literature on social capital in the next section.

2. 4　Social Capital

In order to continue building the theoretical framework on which this research is based, this section presents a review of social capital given its importance as a determinant of innovation. As indicated in Section 2. 1, the appropriate level at which social capital operates is a critical issue. Moreover, "organizations do not behave, people do" (Yuan and Woodman 2010, p. 7); this statement reinforces the fact that firms are shaped by their firm members. Therefore, this section firstly defines social capital at the individual-level, and then, firm-level social capital is represented as contextual effects.

2. 4. 1　Definition of social capital

In terms of defining social capital, as noted by Adler and Kwon (2002), the definitions of social capital have varied according to researchers' different perspectives. Yet a consensus is that the development of contemporary definitions of social capital have largely depended on the pioneering works of Bourdieu (1986) and Coleman (1988). Bourdieu (1986) defines social capital as the sum of the actual and potential resources which are linked with the network of relationships, and also proposes that social capital can exist both at the individual- and group-lev-

el. Coleman (1988) reinforces Bourdieu's relational notion by indicating that social capital is inhered in social relationships, and expands social capital to include
several sub-constructs, such as trust, norms, obligations and expectations. These
sub-constructs are conceptualized in the following section where the social capital's
dimensions are discussed in detail.

A further contribution of Coleman (1988; 1990) is his illustration as to how
social capital relates to other forms of capital. Similar to other forms of capital, social capital is productive. However, unlike human capital, which resides in an
actor, social capital inheres in the relationships held between actors. Compared to
physical and human capital, social capital is much less tangible (Coleman 1990).

Based on the explanation of Bourdieu (1986) and Coleman (1988), many
of the definitions proposed by subsequent researchers contain a resource dimension
that inheres in networks and relationships. For example, Nahapiet and Ghoshal
(1998) define social capital, from a resource-based perspective, as the sum of actual and potential resources located within the network of relationships and the
processes of social exchanges. They also underline that social capital can occur at
the individual-, organizational-, inter-organizational- and societal-level. Furthermore, Lin et al. (2001) suggest that social capital comprises resources which are
embedded in social relations. Baron and Markman (2003) illustrate that social
capital is the actual and potential resource which actors can obtain from knowing
others by being part of a social network.

From the discussion, a striking similarity can be noted amongst a number of
the different definitions, namely that resources embedded in social relations are indeed an important element of defining social capital. In other words, there are a
number of initial and notable scholars, such as Bourdieu (1986), Nahapiet and
Ghoshal (1998), and Lin (2001) who refer to resources such as information,
knowledge, privileges, and support that individuals can only access by and
through relationships. Unlike physical capital (e. g. technology) and human capital (e. g. education), which are the property of actors, the flow of resources a-
vailable to actors is influenced by a network—who interacts with whom, how
frequently, and under what terms (Poder 2011).

Therefore, at the individual-level, for the purpose of this research, social
capital refers to resources embedded in individuals' relationships that are available
to exchange through these relationships. Given that the referent of the construct
in terms of social capital is the individual, the firm-level social capital is identified
as a contextual construct that is aggregated from individual characteristics that are
specific to each individual in the firm. Therefore, the interpretation of firm-level
social capital is based on the aggregation of individual-level social capital (Alexan-

der and Van Knippenberg 2014), referring to the aggregation of resources embedded in the relationships among members of a firm.

2. 4. 2   Three dimensions of social capital

Following the definition of social capital, this section further reviews the conceptualisation of social capital by applying Nahapiet and Ghoshal's (1998) framework, given that this comprehensive definitional framework integrates the extant studies and offers a reasonable conceptualisation that examines social capital as a focal construct (Maurer and Ebers 2006; Zheng 2010). Nahapiet and Ghoshal (1998) have categorized social capital into three dimensions: structural, relational and cognitive dimensions of social capital. The structural dimension reflects the configuration and pattern of relationships between actors, the relational dimension refers to the quality of relationships and the cognitive dimension describes the similarity in terms of languages and visions between actors and between the actor and the network as a whole. This section explores the conceptualisation of social capital, focusing on the three dimensions of social capital from Nahapiet and Ghoshal (1998).

Furthermore, as indicated above, social capital is defined at the individual-level and at the firm-level as the contextual effect. Likewise, the three dimensions of social capital, including sub-constructs of each dimension, are firstly defined and conceptualized at individual-level, and then, the firm-level constructs are represented as the contextual effects that are based on aggregations of individual-level.

1. Structural social capital

The structural dimension is defined as the "overall pattern of connections between actors—that is, who you reach and how you reach them" (Nahapiet and Ghoshal 1998, p. 244). This is related to the structural embeddedness which Granovetter (1992) defines as the mutual contacts between actors. This dimension overlaps with the concept of networks, given that it is always measured by, for example, network size—the number of direct or indirect ties (Burt 1992), and network density which describes the overall connectivity in a network (Yu et al. 2013). Thus, a number of scholars have adopted a network perspective to explore structural social capital (e. g. Burt et al. 2000; Seibert et al. 2001; Marsh et al. 2012; Bizzi 2013).

Within network terminology, an ego is the focal actor within the social network, whereas an alter is an actor to whom the ego connects (Brass 1995). The ego and alter are both termed as nodes, whereby two connected nodes form a dyadic tie and inter-connected ties comprise a network. There are three units of a-nalysis: node, dyadic tie and network. Compared to the measurement in net-work studies (such as network size and network density mentioned above), which mainly focus on the network unit of analysis (Bo and Nielsen 2009), a key issue in the use of structural social capital is related to how to best measure the dyadic tie between two actors (Lechner et al. 2010).

Tie strength is one of the most frequently studied variables, referring to the nature of a relational contact that combines the "amount of time, the emotional intensity, the intimacy and reciprocal services" associated with the tie (Granovet-ter 1973, p. 1361).

Strong ties need intensive interactions, which can promote the willingness to encourage collaborative activities and social cohesion (Coleman 1988; Reagans and McEvily 2003). By contrast, Granovetter's (1973) approach to the concep-tualisation of social capital lies in the strength of weak ties, focusing on the strength of the social ties used to obtain valuable resources. He supports the no-tion that weak ties can best develop social capital, because strong ties tend to bind similar people, such as close friends and family members, in long-term and in-tense relationships, which might preclude access to useful and critical resources. Thus, his weak ties theory supports a position whereby actors can best develop social capital following weak ties with others. However, as Monsted (1995) con-cludes, one of Granovetter's main problems in defining strong and weak ties is that he only focuses on the frequency of contacts, whilst neglecting other aspects of the relationships, including the age of ties.

For the purpose of this research, tie strength is measured at both individual- and firm-level. At the individual-level, tie strength measures the connection be-tween two individuals. The aggregation of dyadic relationship between two indi-viduals forms the firm-level tie strength, which describes the strength relationships among individuals within the firm.

2. Relational social capital

The relational dimension of social capital describes the quality of relation-ships, which can be linked with Granvotter's (1973) concept of relational em-beddedness, referring to the relationships between individuals that have developed through a history of interactions. This section discusses trust and norm of reci-procity as the sub-constructs of relational social capital, as they are the central components of relational social capital and the most significant influencers of inno-vation (Zheng 2010; Kiersch and Byrne 2015).

Trust refers to the belief that the results of another individual's intended ac-tion will be appropriate from one's own perspective (Misztal 1996). It is the most discussed sub-construct of relational social capital, because trust essentially represents the quality of the relationship among actors (Moran 2005; Kemper et al. 2011). Individuals often require resources that belong to others, thus some extent of uncertainty is natural. Therefore, Coleman (1988; 1990) firstly emphasizes the value of trust as a part of social capital to facilitate an exchange. Subsequently, trust is believed to play a strong role in accessing and sharing knowledge, innovative performance, career performance and collaboration (Tsai and Ghoshal 1998; Moran 2005; Reiche 2012). Moreover, the positive outcomes of trust have been widely studied within existing empirical research, at different levels from countries to individuals. For example, having examined the relationship between general trust and innovation at the societal-level across 59 different countries, Dakhli and Clercq (2004) find that trust is positively associated with a country's innovativeness. Similarly, trust between different business units in organizations is positively related to the performance of new products (Rodriguez et al. 2007).

At the individual-level, trust exists between two individuals who have direct positive expectations regarding the goodwill and competence of one another (Maurer et al. 2011). Within an organizational context, both employees and managers with a high-level of trust with their contacts can be more creative and innovate more in processes and products (Lee and Choi 2003; Moran 2005).

More importantly, trusting relationships are rooted in value congruence, in terms of the compatibility of individuals' values with a firm's values (Tsai and Ghoshal 1998). At the firm-level, trust, as the contextual effect, is the expectation aggregated by involved individuals within a firm regarding the goodwill and competence of other members. Within an organizational context, trust is important in shaping reliable and socially accepted behaviour among members within an organization (Hashim and Tan 2015).

Norm of reciprocity refers to the exchange of resources being mutual and perceived as fair (Chiu et al. 2011). In other words, it is an obligation for individuals to return in kind what they have received from others. At the individual-level, the work of Gouldner (1960) is one of the most frequently cited articles on reciprocity. He identifies that the first trusting act shown by an individual in a potential relationship is encouraged by norm of reciprocity, which may reduce the risk that this individual's effort will be taken advantage of. Moreover, every action after this effort can be considered a reciprocal response to prior actions. Coleman (1988; 1990) first identifies reciprocity as an essential component of social capital, arguing that social capital constitutes trust, reciprocity, obligation and expectations. To be specific, the operational principle of these social capital elements resonates with Gouldner's (1960) explanation, namely that if individual A offers resources to individual B and trusts B to reciprocate in the future, this establishes an expectation in A and an obligation on the part of B (Coleman 1990). Accordingly, it follows that where there is social capital, the norm of reciprocity acts as an expectation and obligation between two individuals.

At the firm-level, the norm of reciprocity represents the value aggregated by involved individuals within a firm regarding the mutual and fair exchange among firm members. The shared value of exchange in the firm can lead to salient subjective norms regarding reciprocity. The firm-level norm of reciprocity guides individuals' behaviour by providing an organised and interpretable set of informational cues for individuals working in the firm about what should be avoided and what is considered to be appropriate (Yu et al. 2013).

Nahapiet and Ghoshal (1998) have summarised in their seminal research that the relational dimension is widely discussed with a focus on the personal aspects of network relations in terms of trust, norms, obligations and identification. However, in most existing social capital empirical studies, norms are usually regarded as part of the organizational control system (Zheng 2010), and have always been examined and measured explicitly with the organizational characteristics (e. g. Rass et al. 2013; Cao and Lumineau 2015; Son et al. 2017). As the focus here is on social capital at the individual-level and then to aggregate to form the contextual construct at the firm-level, this study therefore identifies the norm of reciprocity which can be perceived by individuals and aggregated into the firm-level, as a more specific sub-construct of relational social capital.

Moreover, Nahapiet and Ghoshal (1998) also include obligations and identification as the sub-constructs of the relational social capital. However, such sub-constructs are not identified in this study, given that identification implies individuals perceive themselves as one with another individual or a group. This actually emphasizes the similarity between individuals and between the individual and group, thus largely overlapping with the cognitive dimension of social capital. Moreover, as indicated above, an individual's obligation can be categorized into norm of reciprocity, given that the norm of reciprocity acts as an obligation and expectation between two individuals. Therefore, this research only discusses trust and norm of reciprocity as the sub-constructs of relational social capital, and these two sub-constructs will be identified as independent variables to develop the conceptual model in the next chapter.

3. Cognitive social capital

The third dimension of social capital is called cognitive dimension, which is embodied in shared cognition, facilitating a common understanding (Nahapiet and Ghoshal 1998). *Shared cognition* refers to the extent to which individuals in networks can understand and interpret behaviours similarly (Li et al. 2013). Accordingly, two major manifestations of shared cognition are shared language and shared vision. Shared language includes, yet goes beyond, language itself (e. g. English and Chinese), given that it also deals with "the acronyms, subtleties, and underlying assumptions that are the staples of day-to-day interactions" (Lesser and Storck 2001, p. 836). Shared vision embodies the common goals and aspirations of the individuals in a network (Tsai and Ghoshal 1998).

At the individual-level, shared cognition refers to an individual's perception of interpersonal similarity in terms of values and visions with another individual. When two individuals engage in communication (e. g. discussion, questioning, and exchange of information), shared language is a direct and important tool which can influence their perception by evaluating the likely merit of exchange and combination of resources with others (Nahapiet and Ghoshal 1998). Regarding shared vision, it facilitates a common understanding between two individuals about how to interact with others, promoting a meaningful and effective communication by avoiding misunderstanding. In addition, without the perception of interpersonal similarity which is stimulated by the individual's goal and aspiration, individuals are likely to experience "internal conflict" and "cognitive dissonance" (Yu et al. 2013, p. 783). In contrast, the perceived similarity between two individuals can reduce their psychosocial discomfort and conflict which arise from their cognitive disparity (Borgatti and Cross 2003; Makela et al. 2007).

At the firm-level, shared cognition is an aggregation of firm members' cognition in terms of shared language and shared vision. The shared cognition at firm-level helps individuals to predict the needs of the firm and adapt to changing their own demands, as well as shape their perceptions and job-related behaviours (Leana and Van Buren 1999; Mohammed and Dumville 2001; Yu et al. 2013). Thus, firm-level shared cognition can facilitate individuals in understanding the meaning of collaboration among individuals within the firm. However, the shared vision can be seen as a collective norm, namely a binding force which may guide individuals to leave their own interests for those of the firm (Coleman 1988).

In summary, this section conceptualizes social capital by applying Nahapiet and Ghoshal's (1998) framework in terms of structural, relational and cognitive dimensions of social capital. Similar to the approach adopted when defining social capital, the sub-constructs of each dimension are defined at individual-level first, and subsequently at the firm-level as contextual effects. Every sub-construct is discussed in detail and will be identified as the independent variables in the next chapter to develop the conceptual model.

2. 5   Social decision-making constraints as a negative consequence of social capital

Social capital is a coin with two sides (Portes and Sensenbrenner 1993; Adler and Kwon 2002). In addition to the positive consequences of social capital, which have been strongly emphasized by prior studies, it is essential not to ignore the negative outcomes of social capital. Although the negative outcomes of social capital have been mentioned in the literature (Adler and Kwon 2002; Villena et al. 2011), the number of studies investigating a specific negative outcome of social capital as a barrier to impede innovation remains limited. Therefore, this section specifically examines social decision-making constraints, given that it has detrimental effects on creating and applying new ideas (Amabile 1996). The identification of the social decision-making constraints is indispensable for understanding and evaluating social capital more objectively when investing in it, thereby enabling firms to overcome this barrier to innovation.

This section firstly provides the definition of social decision-making constraints at the individual-level and at the firm-level as a contextual effect. Secondly, building on the information provided in Section 2. 4, this section also presents a discussion on various determinants of social decision-making constraints through the lens of social capital.

2. 5. 1   Definition of social decision-making constraints

Constraints can be defined as "a state of being restricted, limited, or confined within prescribed bounds" (Rosso 2014, p. 3). This definition has three characteristics. Firstly, it is relatively broad, which does not limit the source of the constraints. For example, the constraints may arise from an external environment, such as time, resources, and finance, while it may also arise from internal sources, such as intrinsic motivation. Secondly, although only negative consequences are investigated in this research, this definition takes a neutral stand, allowing for the possibility that constraints may have both positive and negative consequences (Rosso 2014). Thirdly, this definition indicates that the constraints are a purposed process with intentional bounds. For example, time constraints can be defined as the factors introduced by time pressures, such as deadlines, which are intended to control individuals' engagement in finishing their work by a certain time. Setting a deadline is a purposeful behaviour which may contribute to the purpose of efficient work and individual creativity (Ohly et al. 2006).

However, apart from intentional constraints, there are some constraints that operate unconsciously. Burt (1992) describes network constraints as the extent to which a network is concentrated in redundant contacts. The purpose of investing in direct or indirect ties is to access more information and resources, thus improving performance. Nevertheless, networks with more strongly interconnected contacts may generate conditions of dependency on others, which in turn, create a state of constraining individuals' perception of autonomy (Bizzi 2013). Such network constraints are unconscious and without deliberate intent, and may have negative consequences. The above is also applicable to social decision-making constraints. The purpose for both individuals and firms in building social relationships is to access, obtain or exchange the resources embedded in those relationships, not to control their behaviours in a task. However, along with the resources, such social relationships also impose some amount of controls on individuals' behaviours, such as discretionary decision-making. It is an unconscious phenomenon, but one that cannot be neglected.

As with social capital, the construct of social decision-making constraints is in need of definition at both levels. Accordingly, at the individual-level, social decision-making constraints can be defined as the individual's perception regarding the extent to which factors introduced by social relationships can control his/her decision-making in undertaking a task. Two aspects can be derived from this definition. Firstly, such constraints occur unconsciously, arising from the individual's social relationships. Secondly, this definition emphasizes the decidedly negative consequence in terms of the sacrifice of decision-making freedom.

As a contextual effect, the firm-level construct is based on the aggregation of the individual-level perceptions. Therefore, social decision-making constraints at the firm-level refer to the aggregated perception of involved individuals within the firm regarding the extent to which factors introduced by social relationships can control their decision-making in undertaking a task.

2. 5. 2   Determinants of social decision-making constraints

The previous section provides the definition of social decision-making constraints, and points out that such constraints, which are embedded in social relationships, are unconscious and have negative consequences. This section explores two main determinants of social decision-making constraints from the perspective of social capital.

The first determinant of social decision-making constraints is network conformity. From the perspective of social capital, individuals within the firm necessarily create demands for conformity (Portes and Sensenbrenner 1993). Social capital makes the resources and information embedded in a specific relationship a-vailable, but it is not free to offer the resources and information. Thus, such so-cial capital also creates the enforcement of the shared vision and norm of reciproci-ty. A shared vision, the manifestation of cognitive social capital that emphasizes the similarity in terms of vision between individuals and between the individual and the firm as a whole, is a binding force that leads to conformity (Tsai and Ghoshal 1998; Lechner et al. 2010). At the individual-level, a shared vision can reduce the likelihood of conflicts between individuals, inducing a routine and al-gorithmic approach to decision-making and problem solving, and thus results in loss of independent judgment (Johnson et al. 2005). At the firm-level, the shared vision provides a referent frame of common understanding of the firm's collective goal, increasing the commitment to exploit synergies (Villena et al. 2011). Therefore, a shared vision (with another individual or the firm as a whole) may constrain the freedom of an individual to make a decision by making concessions to other individuals' interests or to the collective goals, thus failing to pursue their own self-interests (Tsai and Ghoshal 1998).

In addition, as mentioned previously, individuals offer resources to others based on the expectation and obligation that they will reciprocate in the future (Coleman 1990). However, given that reciprocity consumes time and resources, individuals may expect such giving back from others even though their substantive contribution to others has been relatively low. Likewise, at the firm-level, norm of reciprocity represents the value aggregated by involved individuals regarding the mutual and fair exchanges in the firm, which may force individuals to assist others or attend to others' demands even when individuals only expect few benefits from future exchanges (Villena et al. 2011). These situations excessively take advan-tage of the norm of reciprocity. Yet, disrupting relationships because of the un-necessary obligation may generate a negative reputation for the disruptor as a relia-ble partner for future relationships with others in the firm (Gulati 1995). There-fore, due to the necessity of network conformity, the norm of reciprocity may develop some degree of unnecessary obligation that commits resources and con-strains the effective actions and decisions beyond what would be optimal or even derail original goals (Hansen 1999; Malhotra 2004; Lechner et al. 2010).

The second determinant of social decision-making constraints is the hierarchi-cal structure. Within the context of the firm, individuals in higher positions (for example, the central or brokering position) can provide resources that are more valuable. Similarly, an individual with more valued resources can find himself/herself in a higher and more powerful position, such that he/she can "exercise authority" over another individual in a lower position (Lin 2001, p. 35). In addition, the enforceable norms and procedures in the firm are usually approved by those individuals in higher positions. Therefore, in a hierarchical structure, the person in a higher position can constrain the behaviours of another person holding a less powerful position by employing power and command.

Even though a hierarchical structure is a simple formal structure in a firm, the extent of social decision-making constraints is based on how individuals view distinction arising from status (Kemper et al. 2011). Therefore, the second determinant of social decision-making constraints in terms of hierarchical structure is related to cultural issues, which will be discussed in detail in the next section.

2. 6   Culture

The previous sections discussed the conceptualizations of innovation and social capital, as well as a specific negative outcome of social capital in terms of social decision-making constraints. This section reviews related literature on culture, given that culture has been identified as a major environmental characteristic that can shape innovation practice and affect innovation performance through individuals' underlying values and behaviours (Webster and White 2010; Holt 2012). Specifically, as alluded to in the last section, given that one determinant of social decision-making constraints is related to cultural issues, the effect of social capital on social decision-making constraints can be strengthened or weakened by individuals' cultural values.

2. 6. 1   Definition of culture

Culture has been broadly treated as synonymous with the beliefs and values of people, which has not perceptibly changed over the decades (Hofstede 1980). However, this conceptualisation is insufficient for researching the relationship between culture and social capital. Indeed, culture has been defined through many conceptualizations within the management literature. These include culture as "the values, beliefs, norms and behavioural patterns of a nation group" (Leung et al. 2005, p. 357), which exemplifies culture at the national or societal level, and "the software of the mind" or "collective programming of the mind that distinguishes one group of people from another" (Hofstede 2001, p. 9), which exemplifies culture at the individual-level. Moreover, the article by Hinds et al. (2011) about intercultural cross-national collaboration highlights a key distinction among different definitions relating to whether to define culture only by beliefs and values or to encompass the behaviours of individuals. Even though behaviour may not be a part of culture, culture is an important factor in influencing behaviours (Kitayama 2002). As Chao and Moon (2005) argue, culture can be best understood by examining the interrelationship between cultural influences and behaviours. For example, the research by Morris et al. (2008) concerning networks of relationships reveals that Chinese employees are more oriented towards formal superiors due to the influence of Confucian culture, whereas Americans are comparatively transitory because such interactions are shaped in the image of market transactions. Accordingly, the word "culture" not only needs to reflect the relatively homogeneous characteristic, but also needs to express that the cultural context within which the individuals are embedded can influence these behaviours.

The emphasis in this study is placed on social capital at both the individual- and firm-level, for the purpose of considering the potential moderating effects of culture on the effects of social capital, and thus, similar to social capital, culture is defined and conceptualized at the individual-level, and as a context construct at the firm-level.

At the individual-level, culture refers to individuals' beliefs, values, attitudes and norms that distinguish one group of individuals from another by influencing their behaviours. The firm-level culture aggregates individuals' perception, referring to the aggregated beliefs, values, attitudes and norms of involved individuals within a firm.

As outlined in the definition at the individual-level, culture can distinguish between individuals from one group to another. Therefore, this study chooses power distance and high-low context as two specific cultural dimensions to characterise individuals according to the distinction between individual's attitudes to the unequal distribution of power, and their communication styles. The following sections (Section 2.6.2 and 2.6.3) conceptualise power distance and high-low context at the individual- and firm-level, and justify the relevance of these two specific dimensions of culture to the examination of social capital and social decision-making constraints.

2.6.2   Power distance

Power distance is the concept which describes the important distinction between individuals' attitudes to the unequal distribution of power. It is one of the five cultural dimensions investigated by Hofstede (1980; 1991) based on a survey involving more than 100,000 employees from IBM subsidiaries in more than 50 countries.

Hofstede's study is at the country-level; therefore, he defines power distance as "the extent to which a society accepts the fact that power in institutions and organizations is distributed unequally" (Hofstede 1980, p. 45). His statistical analysis shows that the worldwide average index score of power distance is 56. The score ranges from 1 to 120, where an index score of power distance greater than 70 is considered as a high power distance and a score below 40 is considered a low power distance.

Since Hofstede' seminal book, *Culture's Consequences: International Differences in Work-Related Values* (1980) has been published, his cultural value framework has been utilized in a wide variety of empirical studies. However, despite the great impact of Hofstede's framework of cultural value, his work has been subjected to a great deal of criticism (Kirkman et al. 2006; Tung and Verbeke 2010). Two of the most significant are that his work has failed to capture the malleability of culture over time, and has ignored the cultural heterogeneity within-countries (Sivakumar and Nakata 2001). In spite of the criticisms, this study explores power distance, which is one of the five cultural dimensions investigated by Hofstede, for a number of reasons as discussed below.

Firstly, rather than developing the up-to-date items to measure Hofstede's cultural dimensions, researchers, unfortunately, tend to use secondary data, falling back on Hofstede's country scores directly (Kirkman et al. 2006). This gave rise to the criticism that Hofstede's (1980) work fails to capture current cultural value since his data was collected forty years ago. By contrast, this research explores social capital at the individual- and firm-level. Power distance, as one of the moderators, is expected to moderate the relationship between social capital and social decision-making constraints. For the purpose of this research, power distance is conceptualized and measured at the individual- and firm-level, rather than using Hofstede's (1980) country-level score directly. Therefore, this study adopts power distance as the moderator through the use of up-to-date primary data (see Section 4.2 for details on the data collection and Section 4.4 for specific measures), instead of Hofstede's data from 1967 to 1973.

Moreover, the research context of this study is focused on one country—China. The dearth of studies exploring within-country variation can be addressed by measuring individualized power distance in the Chinese context. Therefore, the conceptualisation of power distance is discussed as follows.

Similar to the definition of power distance at the country-level provided by Hofstede (1980), power distance at the individual-level refers to the extent to which an individual accepts the fact that power in institutions and organizations is distributed unequally (Clugston et al. 2000).

Inside a firm, the hierarchical structure is a formal structure. Power distance focuses on the nature of an individual's relationships in terms of hierarchy. How individuals view power relationships can affect how they act in a business context, as superiors and as subordinates. Employees in a position with a low power distance are less conscious of the distinctions arising from status positions and value e-qual participation in making decisions.

By contrast, employees with high power distance are more aware than others about the hierarchy and authority of superiors and how their behaviours should properly reflect the status differences during interactions, thereby, respecting and obeying the power gap with their superiors (Farh et al. 2007; Atwater et al. 2009; Lian et al. 2012). Employees expect that ideas should be given by their superiors, rather than their subordinates. Additionally, employees do not want to challenge their superiors but simply obey all their superiors' decisions or instructions without questioning them (Liu and Liao 2013).

With the consideration of parallel connection between power distance and social capital at both individual- and firm-level, power distance is in need of conceptualisation at the firm-level. Hofstede (1980) discusses power distance in an aggregate sense to characterise differences across nations' cultures. In this vein, firm-level power distance refers to the perception aggregated by involved individuals within the firm regarding their attitudes to the unequal distribution of power.

Even though every individual in the firm is not likely to hold a given shared perception to the same degree, if a sufficient number of firm members subscribe to the values, certain behaviour patterns may become acceptable or critical to the firm (Yang et al. 2007). Furthermore, according to Moreland et al. (2001), individuals, especially newcomers, learn how to respond to the authority relationships, especially that of their supervisor, partly by querying and viewing co-workers interactions with authorities. With assimilation, newcomers adopt theirs firm's particular valuation of power distance (Yang et al. 2007).

In a firm characterized by high power distance, the differences in status and power are not diminished but rather acknowledged and emphasized, as these differences are an integral part of the firm. Most employees refer to each other by their title and last name, such as Manager Zheng and Secretary Shen, to underline the status distinctions and avoid informalities. By contrast, in a firm with low power distance culture, subordinates might address higher status individuals by their first name. In addition, discussions on policies and assignments are more commonplace among members within the firm.

Compared to the norms of a low power distance culture, which may reduce the differences among individuals in positions of different levels of decision-making power, the difference in decision-making power in the firm with high power distance culture is legitimized between those who are in high power positions versus those in low power positions (Madlock 2012). Specifically, a subordinate may simply acknowledge the power of his/her superior merely based upon their relative position in the hierarchy of authority. Decisions are usually made by superiors, which are seldom questioned and are followed by their subordinates because their role in the hierarchy is to follow their superiors.

As indicated above, how to view the relationship in terms of hierarchy is one of the determinants of social decision-making constraints. Therefore, the effects of social capital on social decision-making constraints can be weakened or strengthened with the various extents of power distance. The moderating effect of power distance will be explained in the next chapter.

2. 6. 3   High-low context

In 1976, Edward T. Hall, an anthropologist, differentiated cultures by context. This became one of the most notable cultural classifications (James S Coleman 1988). Context is defined as the "information that surrounds an event" (James S Coleman 1988, p. 200). Hall (1976, p. 101) states that the context of communication between two individuals is critical given that "what one pays attention to or does not attend is largely a matter of context". The elements of context include the environment, setting the background in which the communication takes place, as well as the values, status in society and the relationship among the interacting parties.

Scholars traditionally treat high-low context as a national-level characteristic in cross-culture studies (e. g. Amason 1996; Alattar et al. 2016; Yates and Oliveira 2016). Classically, East-Asian countries (e. g. China, Japan and Korea) are considered as high context countries, whereas Western countries (e. g. United States, Germany and Canada) are categorized as low context countries (Savani et al. 2008). However, the concept of high-low context seems to have lost some of its popularity in recent years due to dubious country classifications attached to the concept (Xiao and Su 2004). The review by Kittler et al. (2004) on the use of high-low context in cross-cultural research fails to find a consistent and empirically well-founded country classification. On the contrary, all studies that utilized high-low context country classifications are based on less-than-adequate evidence (Elke U Weber et al. 2005). Therefore, instead of relying on the existing debatable country-level classification, this study focuses on the cultural variation within a country.

Initially, Hall (1976) proposed high-low context in order to characterise individuals according to the styles in which they communicate by referring to the extent of these non-verbal contexts. At the individual-level, people tend to communicate in an implicit way which can be categorized as high context communication styles. The high context offers the perspective whereby individuals are likely to talk based on context in an implicit way and expect the listeners to infer meaning in light of the context. By contrast, individuals tend to communicate in an explicit way to show their inner thoughts directly with less contextual background, which is called low context.

As with social capital and social decision-making constraints, high-low context needs to be conceptualized at the firm-level as a contextual construct. In general, high-low context at the firm-level is *the aggregation of individuals' communication styles within a firm*. The firm-level concept of high-low context summarises how individuals in a culture relate to others (Kim et al. 1998). In a firm with a high context communication style, more implicit information is carried in the message itself and the message includes other communicative cues which are not uttered (Rosenbloom and Larsen 2003; Würtz 2005). Consequently, a firm with a high context culture is one in which individuals are deeply involved with each other, so that information can be widely shared through simple messages with deeper meaning. The underlying reason for high context is the existence of a structure of social hierarchy (Kim et al. 1998). Individuals' inner feelings are kept under strong self-control due to the top-down decision-making process. Moreover, individuals are deeply involved with others, which may lead to an emphasis on conformity. Consequently, individuals tend not to voice their inner thoughts directly, because careful thought is given to whether and how the words used will influence their relationships with others.

By contrast, in the firm with low context culture, individuals' communications are more explicit, and the information is contained in the message itself (Rosenbloom and Larsen 2003). Individuals are relatively little involved with others and highly individualized. Therefore, social hierarchy and conformity impose less on individuals' lives. Individuals are likely to rely almost solely on the information contained in the message itself, so that the message needs to be explicit and detailed.

In summary, this section discusses power distance and high-low context at the individual- and firm-level. Both of these two constructs will be identified as the moderating variables in the next chapter in order to build a comprehensive conceptual model.

2. 6. 4   The cultural variance within-country

As can be seen from Figure 2. 2, Hofstede's power distance index score reveals that China belongs to a high power distance culture with a power distance score of 80. Even though Hall's (1976) seminal book, Beyond Culture, did not directly identify China as a high context society, subsequent studies adopted his framework to theoretically and empirically confirm that China is a high context country (e. g. Kim et al. 1998; Leets 2003; Koeszegi et al. 2004). This is due to the influence of Confucianism in Chinese culture, which believes in harmony in society through respect for age and social hierarchy (Jandt 2003). Chinese social norms start with the filial responsibility of sons to fathers, and spill over into other hierarchical relationships, such as subject-to-emperor, which provides a model for interaction between student and teacher in school, as well as subordinates and superiors in firms (Morris et al. 2008).

However, even though this study is conducted in a high power distance and high context country, there is considerable variance within-country on such dimensions (Vidyarthi et al. 2014). This is due to the fact that the geographic differences and difference in economic systems employed in China can make for diversity. After the reform and opening up in 1978 and the joining of the World Trade Organisation (WTO), China has grown rapidly into an important economic power with significant international trade volumes and foreign direct investments (Zhang et al. 2013). A growing number of Chinese academics and executives receive their graduate degrees in Western countries which can be categorized as low power distance and low context. As a result, individuals' cultural values are largely based on Confucianism and emphasize traditional Chinese values, but also with strong influence from Western culture (Schyns and Sanders 2006; Liden 2012).

Therefore, taking the within-country variance into consideration, the power distance and high-low context should be measured at the appropriate level of specificity (Liden 2012). As this study explores social capital at the individual- and firm-level, and expects the moderating effects of culture on social capital and its negative consequence, rather than assuming homogeneity among all members of a society, this study measures power distance and high-low context at the individual-level to highlight existing within-country variance.

2. 7　China as the research context

Social capital theory was developed in the West. It has been well supported in much of the research conducted in Western countries, such as the United States and the United Kingdom.

However, there are only a few studies that empirically test social capital in China (Xiao and Tsui 2007; Wu 2008; Li et al. 2013; Yu et al. 2013). Elliot and Nakata (2012) propose that constructs impacting innovation management may differ dramatically in different cultural contexts. Thus far, in the literature review, it appears that social capital is empirically robust. That is, the articles from Xiao and Tsui (2007), Li et al. (2013), Wu (2008) and Yu et al. (2013) indicate robust factor analysis results.

As most studies to date have been extensively undertaken in Western countries, their outcomes and findings are limited in terms of generalizability. As a relationship-rich society (Kogut and Zander 1992), China can provide an interesting context for testing social capital theory, thus contributing significantly to the understanding of social capital theory. Therefore, a study in a non-Western context, such as China, can help to test the generalizability of existing social capital theories, which are largely Western in origin (Gómez-Mejía et al. 2007; Wu 2008). Conducting the study in China is more likely to generate meaningful and lasting implications for academia and practitioners alike (Berrone et al. 2016).

In addition, after joining the WTO, the cultural values in China are increasingly diverse, ranging from traditional Chinese cultural values to international cultural influences from developed economies (Schyns and Sanders 2006; Liden 2012). This diversity in cultural values provides a suitable context in which to test within-country variation in culture, as stated in Section 2. 6. 4.

2. 8　Conclusion

This chapter has offered a deep and detailed treatment of the theoretical foundation of this study. The importance of providing a better understanding of the potential negative outcome associated with social capital and the lack of empirical evidence on how social capital negatively influences firm innovation have inspired this study to focus on this literature. The literatures on innovation, social capital, social decision-making constraints and culture have been examined, which provide a basis for the conceptual model in the next chapter.

In order to offer a comprehensive understanding of firm-level innovation, this research adopts a multilevel analysis. Before providing a review of the litera-ture on specific constructs, Section 2.2 clarifies the theoretical bases of analysis level. Given that innovation is conceptualized at the firm-level, and with the consideration of the nesting nature of firms, constructs of social capital, social de-cision-making constraints and culture are first and foremost defined and conceptu-alized at the individual-level, and properly aggregated as contextual constructs at the firm-level.

Innovation is conceptualized at the firm-level solely. Section 2.3 firstly re-views the literature on firm-level innovation as a process with evolutionary mod-els, and as an outcome with different classifications. Subsequently, drawing on the literature, the definition and classification of innovation is provided in order to establish a clear understanding of the construct underlying this study. In the next chapter, firm innovation will be identified as the dependent variable of the con-ceptual model.

Section 2.4 and Section 2.5 provide a deep discussion regarding social cap-ital and one of its negative consequences, in terms of social decision-making con-straints. These two constructs are explored at the individual-level and as contextu-al constructs at firm-level. Section 2.3 includes the synthesis of social capital's def-initions from different scholars, and the detailed explanation of social capital con-ceptualisation by adopting Nahapiet and Ghoshal's (1998) three dimensions—structural, relational and cognitive dimensions. The specific sub-constructs of each dimension have been explored. In Chapter 3, tie strength of the structural dimension, trust and norm of reciprocity of the relational dimension, and shared cognition of the cognitive dimension will be identified as the independent varia-bles in the conceptual model.

Section 2.5 provides the definition and determinants of the social decision-making constraints. As a mediating variable of the conceptual model, how social decision-making constraints influence the relationship between individual- and firm-level social capital and firm-level innovation will be revealed in the next chapter.

Section 2.6 provides a discussion of culture and identifies two specific cultur-al dimensions—power distance and high-low context. Instead of assuming an av-erage tendency of one national culture, this study focuses on intra-country differ-ences. With the consideration of parallel connection with social capital and social decision-making constraints, the definition and conceptualisation are explained at the individual-level and firm-level. The expectation of moderating effects of pow-er distance and high-low context on the relationship between social capital and so-cial decision-making constraints will be explored in Chapter 3. Section 2.7 explains the merits and appropriateness of China as the research context. Section 2. 8 provides a review of previous studies on social capital-innovation relationships.

Additionally, Table 2. 2 outlines the constructs reviewed in Chapter 2, and presents the link between the conceptual reviewing in Chapter 2 and the conceptual model developed in Chapter 3.

Table 2. 2   Summary of Literature Review

Construct	Conceptualisation		Role in the conceptual model	Research Level
Innovation	Four classifications of innovation: product, process, marketing and organizational innovation		Dependent variables	Firm-level
Social capital	*Three dimensions*	*Sub-constructs*	Independent variables	Individual- and firm-level
	Structural	Tie strength		
	Relational	Norm of reciprocity and trust		
	Cognitive	Shared cognition		
Social decision-making constraints	Determinants of social decision-making constraints		Mediator	
Culture	Two specific cultural dimensions: power distance and high-low context		Moderators	

Chapter 3

Conceptual Model and Hypotheses

3. 1   Introduction

This chapter sets out to establish a conceptual model of social capital-innovation relationships with the mediating effects of social decision-making constraints, leading to research hypotheses which are tested in the later stage of this research. The conceptual model and hypotheses are developed by presenting empirical findings from previous studies, as well as using theoretical perspectives that are proposed but not empirically tested.

It is important to note that this research places particular emphasis upon the negative consequences of social capital. Moreover, given that social capital is a multi-dimensional construct, such emphasis has given rise to the focus on the simultaneous effects of different dimensions of social capital on social decision-making constraints. Furthermore, this study has to carefully consider an appropriate conceptualization of firm-level social capital that is based on individual-level social capital. With the consideration of the nesting nature of individuals in firms, social capital resides in individuals' relationships, and then can be aggregated into firms' social capital as contextual effects. Thus, the theoretical model demonstrates the relationship between individual- and firm-level social capital and firm-level innovation along with the mediator in terms of social decision-making constraints at both levels.

The conceptual model is presented in detail in Section 3. 2. Specifically, the relationships proposed in the conceptual model are presented in detail in Section 3. 3 to 3. 5. Section 3. 6 provides the conclusion.

3. 2   Conceptual model

Most previous studies on the relationship between social capital and organization outcomes have identified one construct as the mediating variable (such as resource exchanges, quantity of knowledge sharing, or resource protection) that di-
rects relations to organizational outcomes (e. g. Tsai and Ghoshal 1998; Seibert
et al. 2001; Danchev 2006; Oh et al. 2006; Wu 2008; Chiu et al. 2011). As
demonstrated in Section 2. 5, social decision-making constraints are identified as
one of the negative consequences of social capital that harm the firm's innovation
performance. Therefore, this study focuses on the possibility of an indirect relationship between social capital and innovation with the mediating effects of social
decision-making constraints.

In order to illustrate the positional influence of social capital on social decision-making constraints, as well as the potential risk of social decision-making
constraints to firm innovation performance, a conceptual model is established and
presented in Figure 3. 1.

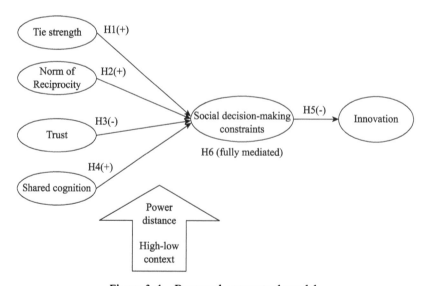

Figure 3. 1   Proposed conceptual model

The conceptual model presented in Figure 3. 1 attempts to provide a holistic
understanding of the negative effect of social capital on innovation, as well as pav-
ing the way for the empirical study in the later part of the research. This model

41

depicts relationships between the main constructs and includes all of the hypotheses formulated in this study.

The central idea of the model is that social capital influences social decision-making constraints, which can impede a firm's innovation. Additionally, the conceptual model also suggests that social capital comprises structural, relational and cognitive dimensions and reveals that sub-constructs of each dimension exert effects on social decision-making constraints. Furthermore, the conceptual model highlights the possible moderating effects of two cultural dimensions, in terms of power distance and high-low context, which may strengthen or weaken the relationships between sub-constructs of social capital and social decision-making constraints.

Furthermore, most previous studies have largely explored how social capital relates to innovation at the same level of analysis, neglecting the multilevel effects of social capital. Therefore, with the consideration of the nested nature of firms where individuals are situated, this study bridges that gap in the multilevel exploration of social capital studies by aggregating individual-level social capital into firm-level as contextual constructs. Thus, a multilevel model is proposed in Figure 3. 1, investigating how individual social capital aggregates within a firm into firm-level social capital, which in turn, influences firm-level innovation.

The multilevel conceptual model (Figure 3. 2) distinguishes the general conceptual model (Figure 3. 1) into two levels in terms of firm-level and individual-level. Therefore, utilizing a multilevel conceptual model for social capital-innovation relationships, this study aims to validate and discuss the proposed relationships at both individual- and firm-level. In the following discussion, this study formulates hypotheses on:

 – How three dimensions of social capital influence social decision-making constraints at the both individual- and firm-level;

 – How social decision-making constraints mediate the relationship between social capital and innovation performance at the firm-level;

 – How culture moderates the relationships between social capital and social decision-making constraints at both individual- and firm-levels.

The specific hypotheses and supporting literature are presented in Table 3. 1, which presents the authors, research context, method of data collection and relevant findings that support the establishment of the research hypotheses. This table aims to assist in determining the possible links and causal relationships between constructs, as well as determining the signs of effect based upon the existing literature within similar research disciplines. In addition, Table 3. 1 also presents the level of analysis and research context of each hypothesis in this study, highlighting

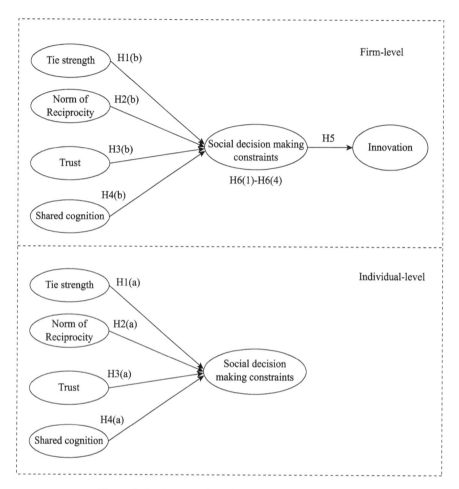

Figure 3. 2   Proposed multilevel conceptual model

the difference from existing studies. Detailed discussion concerning how these constructs could relate to each other, and hence an explanation of each hypothesis contained in the model, is presented in Sections 3. 3 to 3. 5.

Table 3.1   Research hypotheses and the corresponding supporting literature from previous studies

Hypothesis in this research

Hypothesis	Level of analysis	Research context	Positive/negative
H1: Tie strength and social decision-making constraints	Individual and firm	China	Positive

Supporting literature from previous studies

Author(s)	Level of analysis	Research Context	Relevant findings
Perry-Smith (2006)	Individual	Research institute in the U. S.	Strong ties facilitate social influence pressures leading to conformity by leaving little room for autonomy.
Lechner et al. (2010)	Business unit	Large multinational corporations	Further increases of tie strength tend to burden an initiative with social obligations that may detract from goal accomplishment.
Chung and Jackson (2013)	Team	Biology and chemistry research teams	Dense ties may promote mutual interdependence between team members. Strong ties among team members may result in them being more willing to take actions for the sake of the team.

Table 3. 1 Research hypotheses and the corresponding supporting literature from previous studies (continued)

Hypothesis in this research

Hypothesis	Level of analysis	Research context	Positive/negative
H2: Norm of reciprocity and social decision-making con-straints	Individual and firm	China	Positive

Supporting literature from previous studies

Author(s)	Level of analysis	Research Context	Relevant findings
Lechner et al. (2010)	Business unit	Large multinational corporations	Feelings of social obligation can become so strong that ef-fective actions are constrained and original goals derailed in individuals in order to avoid social consequences.
Villena et al. (2011)	Firm	Spanish firms	Reciprocity norms can serve to transform decision-makers from self-centred partners into members of a relationship with shared interests and a sense of the common good. Reciprocity norms may develop unnecessary obligations that constrain choices beyond what would be optimal.

Table 3.1 Research hypotheses and the corresponding supporting literature from previous studies (continued)

Hypothesis in this research

Hypothesis	Level of analysis	Research context	Positive/negative
H3: Trust and social decision-making constraints	Individual and firm	China	Negative

Supporting literature from previous studies

Author(s)	Level of analysis	Research Context	Relevant findings
Molina-Morales and Martinez-Fernandez (2009)	Individual	Spanish firms	Trust, both within and between organisations, has been found to be important to innovation since it lessens the need for rigid control systems.
Li et al. (2013)	Firm	China	Trust helps to lessen the constraints on decision-making
Chung and Jackson (2013)	Team	Biology and chemistry research teams	In a team with a strong internal trust network relationship, team members hesitate to monitor each other's work because doing so may be interpreted as sign of distrust.

Table 3. 1 Research hypotheses and the corresponding supporting literature from previous studies (continued)

Hypothesis in this research

Hypothesis	Level of analysis	Research context	Positive/negative
H4 : Shared cognition and social decision-making constraints	Individual and firm	China	Positive
H5 : Social decision-making constraints and innovation	Firm	China	Negative

Supporting literature from previous studies

Author(s)	Level of analysis	Research Context	Relevant findings
Sutcliffe and McNamara (2001)	Firm	Banks in the U. S.	New behaviours are difficult to establish because insufficient time is spent on cognitive restructuring.
Villena et al. (2011)	Firm	Spanish firms	Parties with similar cognition facilitate individual actions and constrain undesirable behaviour.
Cuevas-Rodriguez et al. (2014)	Firm	Manufacturing and service firms	Social capital can form unwritten norms of conformity that deter individuals from acting in ways that promote innovative activities.
Li et al. (2013)	Firm	China	Due to decision-making constraints, holding innovative ideas is not equal to high innovative performance.

3. 3   The relationship between social capital and social decision-making constraints

As previously mentioned, social capital can make resources and information embedded in the network available to network members; however, it also imposes social decision-making constraints. Accordingly, this section examines the impact of social capital on social decision-making constraints at both the individual- and firm-level.

3. 3. 1   Tie strength and social decision-making constraints

At the individual-level, tie strength measures the strength of the relationship between two individuals. A strong tie between two individuals involves a higher level of closeness and frequent interaction, thus not only making resources and information embedded in the specific relationship available, but also generating conditions of dependence on others (Bizzi 2013) .

For individuals, establishing and maintaining a relationship with others requires investing resources, such as knowledge and time. Dependence arises from investments, because individuals who make investments need to guarantee a return (Berthon et al. 2003) . In particular, maintaining a strong relationship with one another requires much more investment, leading to more dependence. Dependence reduces the perception of individual autonomy, given that it decreases the opportunities for exercising discretionary decision-making (Eranova and Prashantham 2016) . Conversely, if the relationship between two individuals is very distant without frequent interaction, they tend to be independent and may not need to monitor each other's behaviours, leading to more occasions to exert discretion (Clercq et al. 2009; Bizzi 2013) . Bearing the above arguments in mind, Hypothesis 1 is formulated as follow:

Hypothesis 1a: At the individual-level, tie strength increases the extent of social decision-making constraints.

At the firm-level, tie strength and social decision-making constraints are represented as contextual effects. Tie strength at the firm-level measures the strength of the aggregate form of the relationship among all members within the firm. The aggregation of strong ties among firm members involves frequent and close social interactions within the firm, not only permitting firm members to know others and share important information, but can also exercise an aggregate constraining force on discretionary decision-making (Li et al. 2013). Strong ties among firm members promote mutual interdependence, facilitating social influence pressures which leads to conformity by leaving little room for individuals' autonomy (Perry-Smith 2006). Strong ties among individuals within the firm can result in individuals being more willing to take actions for the sake of the firm (Chung and Jackson 2013). This is due to the fact that when individuals with high-level frequency and closeness interact within a firm, it is easier for them to share the information about one of their uncooperative behaviours regarding the violation of network conformity (Maurer and Ebers 2006). Therefore, in order to avoid negative social consequences, the social obligation has to be considered when making a decision (Lechner et al. 2010). Based on the above, this research hypothesis that:

Hypothesis 1b: At the firm-level, tie strength increases the extent of social decision-making constraints.

3.3.2   Norm of reciprocity and social decision-making constraints

At the individual-level, norm of reciprocity represents the exchange of resources between two individuals being mutual and perceived as fair. As previously mentioned in Section 2.3, individuals offer resources to others based upon the expectation and obligation that they can be reciprocated in the future (Coleman 1990). When an individual receives others' resources, they may expect future returns. Thus, the norm of reciprocity may serve to transform the decision-maker from a self-interested individual into a member of a relationship; therefore, such individual's freedom of decision-making can be restricted with the consideration of obligation (Villena et al. 2011).

Furthermore, the norm of reciprocity may develop some degree of unnecessary obligations (Villena et al. 2011). Specifically, it forces individuals to assist others or attend to their demands even when individuals only expect few benefits in the future. Likewise, although individuals' substantive contribution to others has been relatively low, they may still expect great benefits from others' reciprocal services in the future. Moreover, given that reciprocity consumes an individual's time and resources, the unnecessary obligation developed by the norm of reciprocity can commit resources, thus constraining the effective actions or decisions beyond what would be optimal (Malhotra 2004; Lechner et al. 2010; Villena et al. 2011). Therefore, in view of the above discussion, the hypothesis is expressed as follows:

Hypothesis 2a: At the individual-level, norm of reciprocity increases the extent of social decision-making constraints.

At the firm-level, the norm of reciprocity refers to the perceptions aggregated by involved individuals regarding the mutual and firm exchanges among individuals within the firm. The aggregated perception of exchanges among individuals within the firm can infer the prevailing perception in the firm (Richardson and Smith 2007), leading to salient subjective norms regarding reciprocity. The salient subjective norms can guide firm members' behaviours by providing an organised and interpretable set about what is considered to be appropriate and what should be avoided (Yu et al. 2013). Within a firm with a high-level norm of reciprocity, members' feelings of social obligation can become very strong, even though the obligation is unnecessary. Because in a firm, individuals share a value in terms of high-level obligation, disrupting a relationship due to the unnecessary obligation may generate a negative reputation for the disruptor as a reliable partner for future relationships within the firm (Gulati 1995; Reagans and McEvily 2003). Accordingly, this study proposes the hypothesis below:

Hypothesis 2b: At the firm-level, norm of reciprocity increases the extent of social decision-making constraints.

3. 3. 3   Trust and social decision-making constraints

A trusting relationship between two individuals can lead to a strong degree of freedom in making decisions. Individuals' trust occurs when they believe that even if an opportunity exists, the exchange partners should not take advantage of it, which may result in unexpected or even negative consequences. For example, in a trusting relationship, the situation where one individual takes advantage of the norm of reciprocity that produces unnecessary obligations on another individual is unlikely to happen. Therefore, such belief in the good intent and concern of exchange partners is an antecedent to cooperation with taking risk (Nahapiet and Ghoshal 1998).

Moreover, trust indicates a willingness to be vulnerable to others, thus reducing the need for strict control and rigid rules (Molina-Morales and Martinez-Fernandez 2009), which can increase individuals' freedom to make decisions. In an empirical survey involving 158 entrepreneurs in China, (Li et al. 2013) postulate that trust helps to reduce the constraints on decision-making. Hence, the following hypothesis is presented:

Hypothesis 3a: At the individual-level, the trust relationship reduces the extent of social decision-making constraints.

According to Tsai and Ghoshal (1998), trusting relationships are rooted in value congruence, in terms of the compatibility of an individual's value with a firm's value. The firm-level trust refers to the shared expectation of firm members regarding the goodwill and competence of any other members. The lack of trust among firm members results in a harmful climate, whereby the shared perception of possible opportunistic behaviours can result in an increased monitoring of behaviours that constrain every member's exertion of discretion (Song 2009; Bizzi 2013). Conversely, in a trusting environment, firm members hesitate to monitor each other's behaviour and question others daily task and decision-making, because doing so is likely to be interpreted as a sign of distrust (De Clercq et al. 2009; Chung and Jackson 2013).

In addition, there are two types of conflict in the decision-making process, in terms of cognitive conflict and affective conflict. Cognitive conflict focuses on the problem-related differences of opinion which can reduce tension and improve decision quality, whereas affective conflict focuses on individuals or personal issues (Amason and Sapienza 1997; Williams 2015). In a firm with a high-level of trusting relationships among individuals, affective conflicts are likely to be decreased because trust facilitates affective attachments (Yli-Renko et al. 2001). In contrast, the shared perception of firm members regarding cognitive conflict can be created in a firm with high-levels of trust (Morgan and Hunt 1994). Rather than constrain the decision-making, cognitive conflict helps to enhance the understanding when relevant members participate in the decision-making process to express their opinions. The effective use of information from diverse perspectives is likely to be superior to the individual perspectives themselves (Lam and Chin 2005; Li et al. 2013). Moreover, once a trusting environment has been established, even newcomers can also engage in cognitive conflicts, leading to rational thinking, rather than affective conflict. Accordingly, the arguments above lead to the following hypothesis:

Hypothesis 3b: At the firm-level, a trusting environment decreases the extent of social decision-making constraints.

3.3.4   Shared cognition and social decision-making constraints

At the individual-level, shared cognition describes the extent of similarity between two individuals. As Ibarra (1995) states, the common characteristic is the baseline of interpersonal communication, interaction and even attraction. According to self-categorization research, the importance of identification in promoting interactions is emphasized (Hogg and Hains 1996; Reagans 2005). Identification based on a specific attribute may increase the likelihood of relationship development between two individuals who share the same characteristics, because perceived similarity creates opportunities for attraction for one another (Reagans 2005). In this study, two manifestations of shared cognition are shared language and shared vision. Shared language can increase communication efficiency and reduces the probability of misunderstanding (Lechner et al. 2010). Moreover, a high-level of shared vision helps to bring two individuals together by eliminating the possibility of opportunistic behaviour, given that they do not fear others' pursuit of self-interests while compromising a shared goal (M. Aslam et al. 2013).

However, the enforcement of compromise may result in restricting an individual's freedom of decision-making due to the demands of conformity. Furthermore, when two individuals are working together with shared goals, both of them feel the need to know what the other person is doing (Jehn and Mannix 2001). An individual who is observed more is likely to have less occasion to exert discretion (Bizzi 2013). Therefore, high-level shared cognition can exert more restriction on decision-making (Li et al. 2013). As a result of the above arguments, the hypothesis is formulated as follows:

Hypothesis 4a: At the individual-level, shared cognition increases the extent of social decision-making constraints.

At the firm-level, shared cognition is an aggregation of firm members' shared cognition in terms of shared language and shared vision. The firm-level shared cognition can help firm members to shape their perceptions and work-related behaviours by providing a framework for individuals to better understand collective interests and form unwritten norms of conformity (Villena et al. 2011; Yu et al. 2013). In favour of the collective interests and conformity, individuals' actions can be facilitated by the shared cognition to constrain undesirable behaviours (Villena et al. 2011). Thus, in order to achieve the firm's shared goal, firm-level shared cognition increases the commitment to exploit synergies by constraining firm members' freedom to pursue their own self-interests. Moreover, shared cognition can also form unwritten norms of conformity to induce a common "dominant logic" (Cropanzano and Mitchell 2005, p. 183) and any individuals' activities involving significant deviation from the established norm can be deterred, even individuals acting in ways that promote innovative activities (Cuevas-Rodriguez et al. 2014). For this reason new behaviours can be difficult to establish, given that a lot of time needs to be spent on cognitive restructuring (Sutcliffe and McNamara 2001). Accordingly, a shared cognition may create constraints on decision-making by making concessions to the collective interests and the norm of conformity. Hence, this study proposes:

Hypothesis 4b: At the firm-level, shared cognition increases the extent of social decision-making constraints.

3. 4　The relationship between social decision-making constraints and innovation

As outlined in Section 2. 2, innovation can be simply defined as the exploration of new ideas. The four types of firm innovation in terms of product, process, marketing and organizational innovation refer to the successful acceptance and application of creative ideas of new products, process, marketing and organizational methods, respectively. However, due to social decision-making constraints, a creative idea is not equal to an innovative performance. As previously indicated, firm-level social decision-making constraints is not only an aggregate of individual's perceptions regarding the factors introduced by social relationships that control their decision-making, but also plays an essential role in shaping their perception and behaviours when making a decision.

With high-level constraints on decision-making, individuals' creative ideas are likely to be more difficult to be accepted, applied and implemented. For example, in a firm with an environment of high-level constraints, if individuals possess new ideas, they not only need to consider their superiors' view of the application, but also those of their network members. This is due to the fact that short-term sacrifices or significant changes in partners are likely to be necessary for the implementation of such creative ideas to be innovative products, services or systems (Li et al. 2013).

Furthermore, the high-level constraints on decision-making in a firm inhibits intrinsic motivation towards creativity because individuals always have strong desires to maintain their personal ideas and freedom of action (Amabile 1996; Sutcliffe and McNamara 2001). However, many ideas generated by creativity cannot be developed by the individuals who generate them. For example, employees may be highly intrinsically motivated to undertake a new project of their own design, but may be singularly uninterested in the project handed to them by their director.

In conclusion, creative ideas are usually a necessary condition for innovation, but not a sufficient one by themselves, since many creative ideas cannot be developed by individuals who generate them and commercially implemented due to social decision-making constraints.

Although no direct empirical evidence on this relationship is currently available, the study by Li et al. (2013) demonstrates that the constraints on decision-making negatively influences firms' new business development, via a survey on 158 entrepreneurs in China. In light of the above discussion, the hypothesis is formulated as follows:

Hypothesis 5: The extent of firm-level social decision-making constraints is negatively related to firm's innovation performance.

Mediating role of social decision-making constraints

The four hypotheses (Hypotheses 1b, 2b, 3b and 4b) developed above implicitly suggest the relationship between social capital and social decision-making constraints at the firm-level. Hypothesis 5 anticipates the relationship between social decision-making constraints and innovation performance at the firm level. Taken together, whether social decision-making constraints mediate the social capital-innovation relationship warrants an empirical enquiry. Hence, the following hypothesis is proposed:

Hypothesis 6: At the firm level, social decision-making constraints fully mediate the relationship between (1) tie strength, (2) norm of reciprocity, (3) trust, and (4) shared cognition with innovation.

3.5 The moderating effects of power distance and high-low context

Webster and White (2010) demonstrate that culture is the major environmental characteristic that underlies individuals' behaviour and values. Specifically, the extent of the effect of individual social capital on social decision-making constraints can be influenced by local culture. Therefore, this section considers the potential moderating effects of two dimensions of culture, namely power distance and high-low context, on the relationship between social capital and social decision-making constraints.

Power distance focuses on the nature of an individual's perception in terms of hierarchy. Likewise, high-low context not only represents individuals' communication styles, but also emphasizes how individuals relate to others within the social hierarchy. As indicated in Section 2.5.2, the hierarchical structure is one of the determinants of social decision-making constraints, given that the extent of social decision-making constraints is based on how individuals view hierarchy (Kemper et al. 2011). Therefore, the previous relationships between social capital and social decision-making constraints are likely to be moderated by power distance and high-low context.

3.5.1 The moderating effects of power distance

In an organisation, the hierarchical structure is a formal structure, where the manner in which individuals view power relationships can affect how they act as superiors and subordinates in a business context. At the individual-level, power distance refers to the extent to which individuals accept the notion that power in organizations is distributed unequally (Clugston et al. 2000). With a cultural value of low power distance, individuals are less conscious of the differences arising from position status, and they want to participate in the decision-making process equally. By contrast, individuals with a cultural value of high power distance are more aware about the hierarchy and authority of superiors, and they want to simply obey their superiors' decisions without questioning them, regardless of the extent of tie strength, trust, norm of reciprocity, and shared cognition between two individuals. Thus, when the hierarchy is powerful, the effects of social capital on the extent of individuals' perception regarding the constraints on decision-making are less influential. Hence, the following relationships are hypothesised:

Hypothesis 7a: At the individual-level, power distance has a negative moderating effect on the relationships between social capital and social decision-making constraints, such that the relationships between (1) tie strength and social decision-making constraints; (2) norm of reciprocity and social decision-making constraints; (3) trust and social decision-making constraints; and (4) shared cognition and social decision-making constraints are weaker for individuals with the cultural value of high power distance.

At the firm-level, power distance is the aggregated perception of firm members regarding their attitudes to the unequal distribution of power. In a firm with low power distance, the differences among individuals in positions of different levels, including the power of decision-making are likely to be reduced. Conversely, in a firm with high power distance, the difference of power in decision-making between individuals who are in high power positions and in low positions is legitimate (Madlock 2012). Therefore, given that the power is unequally distributed in the firm with high power distance, regardless of what is the extent of social capital (tie strength, norm of reciprocity, trust and shared cognition) among individuals within the firm, decisions are usually made by superiors and are seldom questioned by their subordinates. In short, in a firm with high power distance, the potential effects of social capital on social decision-making constraints are likely to be mitigated. Bearing in mind the argument above, the hypothesis is formulated as follows:

> *Hypothesis 7b: At the firm-level, power distance has a negative moderating effect on the relationships between social capital and social decision-making constraints, such that the relationships between (1) tie strength and social decision-making constraints; (2) norm of reciprocity and social decision-making constraints; (3) trust and social decision-making constraints; and (4) shared cognition and social decision-making constraints are weaker in the firm with the cultural value of high power distance.*

3. 5. 2   The moderating effects of high-low context

Context is "the information that surrounds an event" (James S Coleman 1988, p. 200). High-low context characterizes individuals' communication styles, whereby those with a low context communication style tend to communicate in an explicit way. A low context communication message is one in which the mass of information is vested in the explicit code. Individuals with a low context communication style are likely to communicate most information contained in the message itself in an explicit way (Savani et al. 2008). They are highly individualized, so that social hierarchy and conformity impose less on their lives.

On the other hand, individuals with a high context communication style tend to communicate in an implicit way, where the context surrounding the words plays an important part in the process of communication. A high context communication message is one in which very little of the information is coded and explicit, while most of the information is already in the context. Individuals who value harmony and hierarchical values are often classified as high context communicators (Warner-Søderholm 2013). In order to keep harmony, their inner feelings are under strong self-control and usually expressed directly because they are careful about whether the words can influence their relationship with others. Therefore, if two individuals tend to communicate with high context style, they are deeply involved with each other, which may lead to an emphasis on harmony. Consequently, no matter what the extent of social capital (tie strength, trust, norm of reciprocity and shared cognition) between the two individuals, they usually care about the others' feelings and tend not to voice their inner thoughts directly to avoid conflict and embarrassment (Simons and Peterson 2000), thereby sacrificing the freedom of decision-making. Thus, this study proposes the following hypothesis:

Hypothesis 8a: At the individual-level, high-low context has a negative moderating effect on the relationships between social capital and social decision-making constraints, such that the relationships between (1) tie strength and social decision-making constraints; (2) norm of reciprocity and social decision-making constraints; (3) trust and social decision-making constraints; and (4) shared cognition and social decision-making constraints are weaker for individuals with high context communication styles.

At the firm-level, high-low context is the aggregation of individuals' communication styles within a firm, emphasizing the communication environment of the firm in which individuals reside. In a firm with a high context communication environment, conformity is emphasized. Thus, firm members are deeply involved with each other (Kim et al. 1998), so that information can be widely shared through simple messages with deeper meaning. This leads to a quest for conformity (Klyver et al. 2017), sacrificing the freedom of decision-making in order to keep conformity.

In addition, the underlying reason for high context is the existence of social hierarchy, whereby the top-down decision-making process is more commonplace in a firm with high context culture (Kim et al. 1998). Specifically, in the high context firm, decisions are usually made by superiors, which are seldom questioned by their subordinates due to their role in the hierarchy being to follow their superiors. However, in a firm with a low context communication environment, individuals are less imposed on by social hierarchy and conformity, and thus are highly individualized and relatively minimally involved with others. With the above evidence in mind, the following hypothesis is proposed:

Hypothesis 8b: At the firm-level, high-low context has a negative moderating effect on the relationships between social capital and social decision-making constraints, such that the relationships between (1) tie strength and social decision-making constraints; (2) norm of reciprocity and social decision-making constraints; (3) trust and social decision-making constraints; and (4) shared cognition and social decision-making constraints are weaker in the firm with high context communication style.

3.6   Conclusion

Based upon the review of previous studies of social capital-innovation relationships, this chapter establishes the main conceptual model and research hypotheses. Table 3.2 to 3.4 list all hypotheses in this study. The next chapter will detail the methodology that serves to guide the research approach adopted in this book.

Table 3. 2 **Summary of hypotheses related to social capital—social decision-making constraints—innovation relationship**

H1a	At the individual-level, tie strength increases the extent of social decision-making constraints.
H1b	At the firm-level, tie strength increases the extent of social decision-making constraints.
H2a	At the individual-level, norm of reciprocity increases the extent of social decision-making constraints.
H2b	At the firm-level, norm of reciprocity increases the extent of social decision-making constraints
H3a	At the individual-level, the trust relationship reduces the extent of social decision-making constraints.
H3b	At the firm-level, a trusting environment decreases the extent of social decision-making constraints.
H4a	At the individual-level, shared cognition increases the extent of social decision-making constraints.
H4b	At the firm-level, shared cognition increases the extent of social decision-making constraints.
H5	The extent of firm-level social decision-making constraints is negatively related to the firm's innovation performance.
H6(1)	At the firm-level, social decision-making constraints fully mediate the relationship between tie strength and innovation.
H6(2)	At the firm-level, social decision-making constraints fully mediate the relationship between norm of reciprocity and innovation.
H6(3)	At the firm-level, social decision-making constraints fully mediate the relationship between trust and innovation.
H6(4)	At the firm-level, social decision-making constraints fully mediates the relationship between shared cognition and innovation.

Table 3.3   Summary of hypotheses related to the moderating
effects of power distance

H7a(1)	At the individual-level, power distance has a negative moderating effect on the relationships between social capital and social decision-making constraints, such that the relationship between tie strength and social decision-making constraints is weaker for individuals with the cultural value of high power distance.
H7a(2)	At the individual-level, power distance has a negative moderating effect on the relationships between social capital and social decision-making constraints, such that the relationship between norm of reciprocity and social decision-making constraints is weaker for individuals with the cultural value of high power distance.
H7a(3)	At the individual-level, power distance has a negative moderating effect on the relationships between social capital and social decision-making constraints, such that the relationship between trust and social decision-making constraints is weaker for individuals with the cultural value of high power distance.
H7a(4)	At the individual-level, power distance has a negative moderating effect on the relationships between social capital and social decision-making constraints, such that the relationship between shared cognition and social decision-making constraints is weaker for individuals with the cultural value of high power distance.
H7b(1)	At the firm-level, power distance has a negative moderating effect on the relationships between social capital and social decision-making constraints, such that the relationship between tie strength and social decision-making constraints is weaker in the firm with the cultural value of high power distance.
H7b(2)	At the firm-level, power distance has a negative moderating effect on the relationships between social capital and social decision-making constraints, such that the relationship between norm of reciprocity and social decision-making constraints is weaker in the firm with the cultural value of high power distance.
H7b(3)	At the firm-level, power distance has a negative moderating effect on the relationships between social capital and social decision-making constraints, such that the relationship between trust and social decision-making constraints is weaker in the firm with the cultural value of high power distance.
H7b(4)	At the firm-level, power distance has a negative moderating effect on the relationships between social capital and social decision-making constraints, such that the relationship between shared cognition and social decision-making constraints is weaker in the firm with the cultural value of high power distance.

Table 3.4　　Summary of hypotheses related to moderating
effects of high-low context

H8a(1)	At the individual-level, high-low context has a negative moderating effect on the relationships between social capital and social decision-making constraints, such that the relationship between tie strength and social decision-making constraints is weaker for individuals with high context communication styles.
H8a(2)	At the individual-level, high-low context has a negative moderating effect on the relationships between social capital and social decision-making constraints, such that the relationship between norm of reciprocity and social decision-making constraints is weaker for individuals with high context communication styles.
H8a(3)	At the individual-level, high-low context has a negative moderating effect on the relationships between social capital and social decision-making constraints, such that the relationship between trust and social decision-making constraints is weaker for individuals with high context communication styles.
H8a(4)	At the individual-level, high-low context has a negative moderating effect on the relationships between social capital and social decision-making constraints, such that the relationship between shared cognition and social decision-making constraints is weaker for individuals with high context communication styles.
H8b(1)	At the firm-level, high-low context has a negative moderating effect on the relationships between social capital and social decision-making constraints, such that the relationship between tie strength and social decision-making constraints is weaker in the firm with high context communication style.
H8b(2)	At the firm-level, high-low context has a negative moderating effect on the relationships between social capital and social decision-making constraints, such that the relationship between norm of reciprocity and social decision-making constraints is weaker in the firm with high context communication style.
H8b(3)	At the firm-level, high-low context has a negative moderating effect on the relationships between social capital and social decision-making constraints, such that the relationship between trust and social decision-making constraints is weaker in the firm with high context communication style.
H8b(4)	At the firm-level, high-low context has a negative moderating effect on the relationships between social capital and social decision-making constraints, such that the relationship between shared cognition and social decision-making constraints is weaker in the firm with high context communication style.

Chapter 4

Methodology

4. 1   Introduction

This chapter presents the research methodology that has been employed in this study and is divided into ten major sections. Following the introduction, Section 4. 2 discusses the research design and justifies why fixed design and quantitative methods have been used in this research. Section 4. 3 introduces the administration of the fieldwork. Section 4. 4 develops and discusses the scale items used to determine constructs forming the conceptual model. Section 4. 5 describes the survey used to collect the data, Section 4. 6 presents the process of the translation-back-translation of the survey and Section 4. 7 describes the process of a small-scale pre-test. The execution of the survey is presented in Section 4. 8. Finally, Section 4. 9 concludes the chapter.

4. 2   Research design

The research design is "concerned with turning research questions into projects" (Robson 2002, p. 80), focusing on the relationship between research questions, strategy and methods. The relationship between these three issues needs to be handled in a consistent and systematic manner. According to Robson (2002), the general principle is that the research method and strategy must be appropriate for the research questions to be answered. This study follows Robson's (2002) principle to design the research in a way that fits the research method and strategy to the research questions.

4. 2. 1　Research questions

The main research questions for this study are stated as follows:

What is the mediating role of social decision-making constraints in the relationships between individual- and firm-level social capital and firm-level innovation? How does culture moderate these relationships?

In order to address the research questions, a conceptual model that illustrates the indirect relationships between social capital and innovation via the mediating effects of social decision-making constraints was developed in Chapter 3 (based upon an extensive review of the literature). Overall, the purpose of the current study is to test the conceptual model to identify the mechanism through which individual- and firm-level social capital influences firm-level innovation with the consideration of culture.

4. 2. 2　Fixed design strategy

The current study employs a fixed design as the main research strategy. According to Robson (2002, p. 4), a fixed design means that "a very substantial amount of pre-specification about what you are going to do, and how you are going to do it, should take place before you get into the main part of the research study." He also classifies fixed and flexible designs as alternative classification criteria of research strategies to quantitative and qualitative research. A fixed design is theory-driven, which means that a conceptual model should be developed in advance of the research process. Accordingly, researchers should have a deep conceptual understanding before undertaking the fieldwork. By contrast, flexible design involves less pre-specification, in that it evolves, develops and unfolds as the research proceeds.

Therefore, the current study employs a fixed design to test the conceptual model developed based upon an extensive review of the literature. The conceptual model can be used to guide the data collection, whereby the data is used in turn to examine the relationships presented in the theoretical model.

4. 2. 3　Quantitative method

In this study, a quantitative method using a self-administered survey has been employed to collect data about the underlying constructs proposed in the conceptual model. This section provides a justification for the quantitative method employed, as well as further justifying the use of a survey as being appropriate for data collection.

1. Justification for the use of a quantitative method

According to Neuman (2006, p. 63), a quantitative method can be described as "an organized method for combining deductive logic with precise empirical observations of individual behaviour in order to discover and confirm a set of probabilistic causal laws that can be used to predict general patterns of human activity". Applying a quantitative method can provide statistical evidence concerning the strengths and directions of relationships among constructs (Amaratunga et al. 2002). Hence, this study aims to measure underlying constructs, given that the measurement of constructs is a significant and integral aspect of quantitative research (Cavana et al. 2001). In addition, the quantitative method has been successfully employed in similar social capital-innovation studies (e. g. Tsai and Ghoshal 1998; Landry et al. 2002; Reagans and McEvily 2003; Levin and Cross 2004; Molina-Morales and Martinez-Fernandez 2009; Chiu et al. 2011; Bradley et al. 2012; Li et al. 2013).

Moreover, following the principle from Robson (2002) and Punch (2013), the research method used to conduct the research needs to be in line with research questions that are linked to the research strategy and suitable for data collection. As demonstrated previously, the research questions in this study explore the relationship between social capital and innovation with the mediating role of social decision-making constraints and the moderating effects of culture. A quantitative method is used in this research to empirically investigate causal relationships in the conceptual model and subsequently answer the research question.

The framework for the research design is presented in Figure 4. 1. The conceptual model can be viewed as an intermediary, linking the research question, fixed design (research strategy) and quantitative method (research method). In order to address the research question, this study adopts a fixed design as the research strategy to develop a conceptual model as the pre-specification before the fieldwork, and then employs a quantitative method to collect data to empirically test the conceptual model.

2. Survey as a data collection method

Pérez-González (2006) demonstrate that theory and method are interrelated. They also note that, although this view is widely held, the relationship is complicated and occasionally controversial across various communities of organizational researchers.

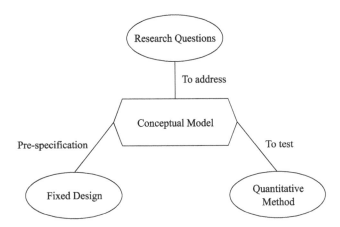

Figure 4.1   Framework for research design

Bennedsen et al. (2007) label the relationship between theory and method as fit. They provide recommendations for the appropriate methods when the theoretical development of a research area is in the mature stage. Research in the mature stage "leads to further refinements within a growing body of interrelated theories" (Bennedsen et al. 2007, p. 1159). As Chapters 2 and 3 have demonstrated, the impact of social capital on innovation management is in the mature stage. According to Bennedsen et al. (2007), the appropriate methods of data collection for the mature stage are survey, systematically coded and quantified interviews/ observation and secondary data.

Secondary data is information or data that has already been collected and recorded by someone else for a different purpose (Gómez-Mejía et al. 2011). For example, the annual reports of public companies and information pertaining to financial markets are widely available and often used as secondary data. However, the main problem with using secondary data is that the data may not fit the requirement of the research questions. Specifically in this study, few public sources provide information regarding firms' innovation performance, and much less regarding employees' relationships with their colleagues and superiors due to the subjectivity of such information. Therefore, using secondary data is not appropriate for this study.

As indicated in the previous section, this study adopts fixed design as the research strategy. Surveys are one of the most commonly used methods of fixed design research (Robson 2002). In particular, a self-administered survey, the data collection method used in this study, can be defined as "a data collection technique in which the respondent reads the survey questions and records his or her own responses without the presence of a trained interviewer" (Hair et al. 2003, P. 265) . The self-administered survey has been used as the data collection method owing to the following advantages.

Firstly, self-administered surveys are relatively cheap to produce and require less time than other data collection methods such as personal interviews. The population in this study requires a large number of respondents; therefore, a self-administered survey can be used to collect data more quickly and economically. Secondly, using self-administered surveys can reach participants who might otherwise be inaccessible. Thirdly, a self-administered survey can provide greater anonymity to the individual respondents. It is quite significant for the current study, given that some sensitive information, such as a firm's innovation performance and employees' relationships with their colleagues and superiors is required.

Another alternative is the use of systematically coded and quantified interviews. However, as with secondary data, the quality of employees' relationships with their colleagues and superiors is difficult to observe. The interview approach potentially could be used. It is, however, prohibitively time consuming and unnecessary, given that self-administered surveys can be used to collect the same data more quickly and with less expense.

For the reasons above, a self-administered survey has been employed to collect the data used to test the conceptual model. The strategy to collect the self-administered survey will be explained in Section 4. 3. 2.

4. 3   Field design

In order to test the conceptual model, this study seeks to collect data in China's Tianjin Economic-Technological Development Area (hereinafter referred to as TEDA) . This research chooses Chinese indigenous high-technology firms less than 10 years old for the following reasons.

Firstly, the review of previous studies on the social capital-innovation relationship reveals that empirical studies of social capital have been primarily undertaken in Western contexts to-date; thus, it remains largely unexplored as to how the mechanisms of social capital operate in indigenous firms in other countries. Therefore, it is appropriate to choose Chinese indigenous firms to test the generality of existing theories developed in Western contexts (Wu 2008) . In addition, Chinese firms have a long tradition of using relational ties to conduct business, despite the increasing prevalence of using contracts (Zhou et al. 2014) .

Secondly, innovation plays a critical role in the successes of high-technology firms. Such firms are fast-growing and characterized by constant innovative activities and thus can provide a proper setting for testing the effects of social capital on innovation (Batjargal 2003b; Uhl-Bien and Maslyn 2003; Taras et al. 2010).

Thirdly, this research selects firms less than 10 years old because individual social capital is seen as an important asset for firms to conduct business during the start-up period (Shane and Stuart 2002; Li et al. 2013). More specifically, new high-tech firms are rarely started by individuals acting in isolation; conversely, they generally involve teams of highly-skilled individuals that have to effectively interact (Anderson et al. 2007).

Finally, TEDA serves as a place where the local high-technology industry can expand. At present, there are 234 Chinese local high-technology firms and 3,734 firms were recognized as small and medium scientific and technology enterprises at the end of 2013 (Gargiulo et al. 2009; TEDA Administrative Commission 2014). Moreover, one of the main advantages in selecting TEDA is that once the researcher has accessed and secured the assistance from some of the high-technology firms, it is very likely that such firms can provide further assistance to gain access to other firms.

4.3.1 Introduction to the Tianjin Economic and Technological Development Area (TEDA)

The China National Economic and Technological Development Areas comprise the special areas of the People's Republic of China in which foreign direct investment is encouraged. Tianjin Economic and Technological Development Area (hereinafter referred to as TEDA), is one of China's first 14 development areas, and was set up in Tianjin Binhai New Area (hereinafter referred to as TBNA) on December 6th, 1984, upon the approval of the State Council.

To date, TEDA has ranked first in the General Evaluation on National Level Development Areas for 17 successive years (1997 – 2013) (Morgeson et al. 2015). TEDA has sustained its leading role among all national level development areas, not only due to its comprehensive investment environment, but also through encouraging local high-technology firms (TEDA Administrative Commission 2014). In China, firms that are recognized as high-technology need to be in the following specific fields: telecommunications, new materials and energy, manufacture of pharmaceutical products, aviation and modern services (Ministry of Science and Technology 2008). Table 4.1 lists these specific industries according to the NACE classification (*nomenclature statistique des activités économiques dans la Communauté européenne*), which is the industry standard classification system used in the European Union.

Table 4. 1   List of industries included in the category of high-tech firms

NACE code	Industry
20	Manufacture of chemicals and chemical products
21	Manufacture of basic pharmaceutical products and pharmaceutical preparations
26	Manufacture of computer, electronic and optical products
27	Manufacture of electrical equipment
28	Manufacture of machinery and equipment
29	Manufacture of motor vehicles, trailers and semi-trailers
30. 2	Manufacture of railway locomotives and rolling stock
30. 3	Manufacture of air and spacecraft and related machinery
51	Air transport
61	Telecommunications
62	Computer programming, consultancy and related activities

Among nine pillar industries in TEDA, six of them can be categorized as high-technology industries, with a turnover of 592 billion Yuan in 2013 and accounting for 73. 5 percent of TEDA's overall production value (TEDA Administrative Commission 2014). Table 4. 2 presents TEDA's five pillar industries according to NACE code, as well as indicating whether each industry belongs to the category of high-tech.

Table 4. 2   List of TEDA's five pillar industries that can categorized as high-tech industry

TEDA's five pillar high-tech industries	According to NACE classification	
	Code	Industry
Telecommunications	61	Telecommunications
Automotive	29	Manufacture of motor vehicles, trailers and semi-trailers
Equipment manufacturing	27	Manufacture of electrical equipment
	28	Manufacture of machinery and equipment
Bio-tech and Medicine	20	Manufacture of chemicals and chemical products
	21	Manufacture of basic pharmaceutical products and pharmaceutical preparations
Aviation	30. 3	Manufacture of air and spacecraft and related machinery
	51	Air transport

In light of the above, TEDA provides a good context in which to test the conceptual model. TEDA has a large number of high-technology firms, which can thus ensure a reasonable sample size for the current study. Additionally, TEDA is one of the largest national-level development areas in terms of revenue generation and investment environment. It has 234 Chinese local high-technology firms and 3,743 small-and medium-sized scientific and technology firms. However, TEDA may not be representative of Chinese national development areas in general. This point is discussed further in Section 7.5 in suggestions for future research. The following section details the strategy for sampling.

4.3.2 Sampling strategy

Snowball sampling is a non-probability sampling technique whereby the researcher starts by collecting data from one or more firms, and using these initial respondents as key informants to identify further respondents (Robson 2002). Although snowball sampling lacks the features of random selection, as outlined below, it is considered the most appropriate technique for the execution of this research.

Snowball sampling is useful when it is difficult to identify members of the population from which respondents are to be drawn. It is for this reason that snowball sampling has been suggested as one of the most effective methods to access hard to reach populations (Zahra and Garvis 2000). In particular, respondents' social networks can be used to identify potential contacts and greatly expand the sample size (Liang et al. 2014). Moreover, snowball sampling is more likely to ensure a better response rate when gaining the initial collaboration from respondents (Kozlowski and Klein 2000). In this sense, snowball sampling can be used to reach a reasonable sample size.

In addition to snowball sampling, this study has applied the key informant method, whereby the respondents in this study that have been chosen are top managers and employees of the sample firms. The key informants in the current research are the top managers in each firm, who are considered the appropriate representative of the corresponding firm to provide data about their firms' innovation performance. According to Leiva et al (2011), top managers are most able to determine and influence a firm's innovation activities. In addition, they can provide reliable information regarding the organizational characteristics and performance of their firms (Batjargal 2003a). Furthermore, as employees have been chosen to answer the questions about their relationships with their colleagues and superiors, top managers are best qualified and most competent to direct surveys to employees within the firm. Moreover, in addition to the dual role of respondents to answer questions regarding firms' innovation performance and to direct the surveys to their employees, top managers also serve the role of a guide to potential new firms for the researcher.

Specifically, in this study data were collected from high-technology firms in TEDA. To begin, face-to-face pilot interviews were undertaken with three top managers in three of TEDA's high-tech firms.

The three top managers served as the starting point for the snowball sample. These managers not only reviewed the survey, but they also helped the researcher to telephone top managers in other high technology firms and asked them to participate in the study. In total, the three managers introduced five managers in other high-technology firms who agreed to participate in this research.

As the key informant, the top manager represented the corresponding firm. Such managers were asked to answer questions about the firm's innovation performance, and help to deliver related surveys to their employees. In addition, the researcher asked whether they would be willing to provide the contact information of top managers in other TEDA high-technology firms. Not every top manager agreed to supply a contact name, but most of them did agree to introduce at least one top manager in other high-technology firms to the researcher. Ultimately, data were collected from 102 firms. The administration of the survey is detailed in Section 4. 8.

4. 4   Scale development

This section explains the selection of scale items used to measure the constructs in this study, which are as follows:

  - Innovation;
  - Three dimensions of social capital: structural social capital (tie strength) , relational social capital (trust and norm of reciprocity) and cognitive social capital (shared cognition) ;
  - Social decision-making constraints;
  - Cultural influences (power distance and high-low context) .

A number of studies provide survey instruments containing operationalised constructs that this study can possibly use. Therefore, in order to adopt high quality existing survey items, the following considerations have been followed. Firstly, so as to ensure the feasibility of the prior instrument to measure the constructs in the current study, items should be used in a similar research field to this study. Secondly, multiple indicator measures should be considered first, given that they can better capture the full concept of constructs, provide comprehensive evaluation and distinguish between different responses. Thirdly, items that have been adopted repeatedly by previous research can enhance replicability. Therefore, such items should be given priority for adoption. Finally, items have to reach an acceptable level of reliability and validity.

As depicted in the conceptual model, the relationship between innovation and social capital has been determined by eight constructs: innovation, tie strength, trust, norm of reciprocity, shared cognition, and social decision-making constraints, as well as power distance and high-low context. Moreover, in testing a model with constructs at two levels (at the individual- and firm-level, as is the case in this study), it is significant to consider the nature of each construct at both levels, and the nature of each effect occurring within or across levels.

As indicated in Section 2.2, given that the level of theory provides justification for the level of measurement of constructs, the level of measurement should be critically aligned with the level of theory. Specifically, four constructs of social capital (in terms of tie strength, norm of reciprocity, trust and shared cognition), the construct of social decision-making constraints, and two moderators (in terms of power distance and high-low context) are identified at the individual-level and at the firm-level as the contextual constructs. Therefore, this study proposes a relatively novel multilevel approach, in terms of multilevel structural equation modelling (MSEM) (Preacher et al. 2010). The key novelty arises from the use of MSEM whereby constructs can be measured at the individual-level and then allowed to vary at both the individual- and firm-level of analysis. The detailed advantage of MSEM and the rationale regarding its use to analyse data are discussed in the next chapter.

Accordingly, the construct of innovation is measured explicitly at the firm-level. The construct of tie strength, norm of reciprocity, trust, shared cognition, social decision-making constraints, power distance and high-low context are conceptualized and hypothesized to exist in some form at the individual-and firm- level, yet all are measured exclusively at the individual-level, given that MSEM can infer the constructs at firm-level based on the individual-level responses.

All the items of each construct used in this study have been developed from a review of the relevant literature. A total of 36 items have been adopted to measure the constructs in the conceptual model, and Table 4.3 reveals a summary of the source of the items of each construct. Moreover, following the discussion and definition of each construct in previous chapters, the operationalisation of measurement of these constructs is discussed in detail below.

Table 4. 3   Total of scale items

Constructs	Number of items	Sources	Level of measurement
Innovation	5	Community Innovation Survey (Central Statistics Office 2012)	Firm
Tie strength	2	Hansen (1999)	
Trust	5	Chiu et al. (2006)	
Norm of reciprocity	2	Wasko and Faraj (2005)	
Shared cognition	5	Li et al. (2013)	Individual
Social decision-making constraints	5	Li et al. (2013)	
Power distance	8	Kirkman et al. (2009)	
High-low context	4	Warner-Søderholm (2013)	

4. 4. 1   Innovation

For the purpose of this research, innovation is defined at the firm-level as the implementation of new products (goods or services), process or marketing and organizational methods in a firm according to the successful acceptance and application of creative ideas. In line with the definition, this research adopts the OECD (2005) methodology to classify innovation according to innovative outputs in terms of product, process, marketing and organizational innovation. Therefore, the construct of innovation is measured with the items adopted by the Community Innovation Survey (Central Statistics Office 2012), which collects information about product and process innovation as well as organizational and marketing innovation during the three year period from 2008 to 2010. Moreover, in the pilot study, with in-depth interviews with three top managers in three high-technology firms, modifications were made to fit the context of the study. For example, instead of asking "During the three year period from 2008 to 2010, did your enterprise introduce new or significantly improved goods?", this research requires respondents to provide precise quantitative data by asking "How many new or significantly improved goods has your firm introduced during the last three years?" This arises because answering "yes" or "no" just provides an answer as to whether the firm has introduced innovation regarding good, services or activities. However, in order to analyse the extent of each firm's innovation performance precise quantitative data are required. Section 4. 7 will provide more details regarding the pilot study. All of the items regarding product, process, marketing and organizational innovation are listed in Table 4. 4.

| Table 4. 4 | Measures of innovation |

Item Label	Adopted Measures from the Community Innovation Survey (Central Statistics Office 2012)
PRODI	How many new products has your firm introduced during the last three years?
PRODI1	*The number of new-to-the-world products*
PRODI2	*The number of new-to-the-firm products*
PRODI3	*The number of major changes to existing products*
PRODI4	*The number of minor changes to existing products*
PROCI	How many process innovations has your firm introduced during the last three years?
PROCI1	*The number of new or significantly improved methods of production*
PROCI2	*The number of new or significantly improved methods of logistics*
PROCI3	*The number of other new or significant improved methods that support process innovation, such as the system of maintenance*
MARKI	How many new marketing methods has your firm introduced during the last three years?
MARKI1	*The number of new or significantly improved packaging or design of a product*
MARKI2	*The number of new methods of promotion*
MARKI3	*The number of new sales channels*
MARKI4	*The number of new price positioning*
ORGAI	How many new systems or programmes has your firm introduced during the last three years?
ORGAI1	*The number of new systems of training*
ORGAI2	*The number of new systems of quality management*
ORGAI3	*The number of new systems of supply chain management*
ORGAI4	*The number of new systems of knowledge management*
ORGAI5	*The number of new systems of external relations management, such as relations with government, public organizations and outsourcing*
ORGAI6	*The number of new systems of managing employees' responsibilities*

4. 4. 2   Tie strength

In this study, tie strength is defined as the nature of relational contact that combines the amount of time and closeness associated with a tie (Granovetter 1973). There are two distinct aspects of tie strength, namely closeness and frequency. Therefore, this study adopts Hansen's (1999) two items of tie strength- the closeness of a working relationship and the frequency of communication- given that these two scale items are consistent with the concept of tie strength as employed in this study. Moreover, according to Hansen's (1999) approach, these two items employ a work-related meaning of closeness in the organizational context (Levin and Cross 2004), which is quite similar in scenario to the current study. Therefore, this study largely retains the original two items, although some slight modifications are made to make the expressions more suitable to the current research and target respondents. Table 4. 5 lists the original and modified survey items.

Table 4. 5   **Measures of tie strength**

Item Label	Adopted Measures	Original Measures
TSC1	How close is your working relationship with the colleague?	How close was your working relationship with each person?
TSS1	How close is your working relationship with the superior?	
TSC2(R)	How often do you communicate with the colleague?	How often did you communicate with each person?
TSS2(R)	How often do you communicate with the superior?	
Note	(R) refers to the reversed score item. Original measures are adopted from Hansen (1999).	

The construct of tie strength has been operationalised using seven-point Likert scales. The item concerning closeness is assessed on a scale ranging from "1 = very distant" (low extent of closeness) to "7 = very close" (high extent of closeness). Furthermore, the item about communication frequency is measured at seven intervals: "1 = daily", "2 = twice a week", "3 = once a week", "4 = twice a month", "5 = once a month", "6 = once every second month", and

"7 = once every three months, less frequently or never". These responses describe the communication frequency from high extent to low extent. Thus, TS2 is the reverse-scored item. The item label should be changed to TS2(R). After the re-coding of items during the data organising, the label can be transferred to TS2.

4. 4. 3 Norm of reciprocity

Norm of reciprocity refers to the exchange of resources being mutual and perceived as fair between two individuals (Chiu et al. 2011), which focuses on the fairness of resources sharing. Wasko and Faraj (2005) develop a two-indicator scale with a seven-point Likert response to measure the construct of norm of reciprocity based upon the theorization of Constant et al. (1996), with a composite reliability of 0. 90. Similar to the current study, the two items of norm of reciprocity from Wasko and Faraj (2005) emphasise the fairness between individuals in the process of sharing knowledge.

Table 4. 6   Measures of norm of reciprocity

Item Label	Adopted Measures	Original Measures
NRC1	I know that the colleague would help me, so it is only fair to help the colleague.	I know that other members will help me, so it is only fair to help other members.
NRS1	I know that the superior would help me, so it is only fair to help the superior.	
NRC2	I trust that the colleague would help me if I were in a similar situation.	I trust that someone would help me if I were in a similar situation.
NRS2	I trust that the superior would help me if I were in a similar situation.	
Note	Original measures are adopted from Wasko and Faraj (2005).	

In addition, by reviewing the relevant literature, it has been found that previous studies used these items to measure norm of reciprocity (e. g. , Chiu et al. 2006; H. Aslam et al. 2013). Therefore, this study adopts the two indicators as per Wasko and Faraj (2005) to measure norm of reciprocity (Table 4. 6). Furthermore, some slight modifications in the wording are made to fit the context of the study.

4.4.4   Trust

In this study, trust is defined as the belief that the results of another individual's intended action will be appropriate from one's own perspective (Misztal 1996). It comprehensively describes the belief in the good intent, concern, reliability and capability among individuals (Nahapiet and Ghoshal 1998). Therefore, the construct of trust is assessed with items adopted by Chui's (2006) measurement, which reflect individuals' belief in others' non-opportunistic behaviour, promise keeping, behaviour consistency and truthfulness.

Table 4.7   Measures of trust

Item Label	Adopted Measures	Original Measures
TRC1	Neither the colleague nor I take advantage of each other even when the opportunity arises.	Members in the BlueShop virtual community will not take advantage of others even when the opportunity arises.
TRS1	Neither the superior nor I take advantage of each other even when the opportunity arises.	
TRC2	The colleague and I can keep the promises we make to one another.	Members in the BlueShop virtual community will always keep the promises they make to one another.
TRS2	The superior and I can keep the promises we make to one another.	
TRC3	Neither the colleague nor I knowingly do anything to disrupt the communication.	Members in the BlueShop virtual community would not knowingly do anything to disrupt the conversation.
TRS3	Neither the superior nor I knowingly do anything to disrupt the communication.	
TRC4	Both the colleague and I behave in a consistent manner.	Members in the BlueShop virtual community behave in a consistent manner.
TRS4	Both the superior and I behave in a consistent manner.	
TRC5	Both the colleague and I are truthful in dealing with one another.	Members in the BlueShop virtual community are truthful in dealing with one another.
TRS5	Both the superior and I are truthful in dealing with one another.	
Note	Original measures are adopted from Chui (2006).	

Using a seven-point Likert response ranging from "1 = strongly disagree" to "7 = strongly agree", Chui's (2006) measurement has been developed to measure the nature of trust among members in a virtual community. In addition, they report a composite reliability of 0.89. Thus, in order to make the items more relevant to the current research, slight modifications in the wording are made. Table 4.7 lists the original and modified items of the construct of trust in detail.

4.4.5 Shared cognition

In this study, shared cognition refers to the extent to which two individuals understand and interpret behaviours similarly. Shared vision and shared language are the two major manifestations of shared cognition. Li et al. (2013) develop a four-indicator scale to measure shared cognition based upon the work of Nahapiet and Ghoshal (1998). They measure the construct of shared cognition using a seven-point Likert response with anchors of strongly disagree to strongly agree, reporting the composite reliability of 0.85.

Table 4.8   **Measures of shared cognition**

Item Label	Adopted Measures	Original Measures
SCC1	The colleague and I use understandable language to communicate with each other.	We share similar language, and I can fully understand what they mean.
SCS1	The superior and I use understandable language to communicate with each other.	
SCC2	The colleague and I prefer to use the same means to communicate with each other (e.g. face to face, text, Email, etc.).	We share similar language, and I can fully understand what they mean (see the note below).
SCS2	The superior and I prefer to use the same means to communicate with each other (e.g. face to face, text, Email, etc.).	
SCC3	The colleague and I have similar interests.	We have similar interests.
SCS3	The superior and I have similar interests.	
SCC4	When working together, the colleague and I share similar goals and principles regarding work-related problems.	We share similar principles regarding how to conduct business.
SCS4	When working together, the superior and I share similar goals and principles regarding work-related problems.	

continued

Item Label	Adopted Measures	Original Measures
SCC5	When working together, the colleague and I share similar values about which behaviour is appropriate or right.	We share similar values about which behaviour is appropriate or right.
SCS5	When working together, the superior and I share similar values about which behaviour is appropriate or right.	
Note	Original measures are adopted from (Li et al. 2013)	

In the current study shared language includes, yet extends beyond language itself; rather, it deals with all the staples of day-to-day interactions (Lesser and Storck 2001). Thus, in order to better reflect the current research, the first original item from Li et al. (2013), "we share similar language, and I can fully understand what they mean" is best divided into two separate items, one relating to "use understandable language" and the other to "use the same means to communicate". Therefore, items SC1 and SC2 are extended from the first single item of Li et al. (2013). Other items are largely adopted from the original items of Li et al. (2013), albeit in a reworded form to make the scale fit the current study.

4.4.6 Social decision-making constraints

Social decision-making constraints refer to one of the specific negative outcomes of social capital, which can be defined as the extent to which factors introduced by social relationships can control individuals' decision-making in undertaking a task. Li et al. (2013) develop initial scale items of the construct according to their in-depth interviews and revise such items based upon the work of Adhikari and Goldey (2010). Finally, in their study, five items are developed to ask their respondents to assign a seven-point Likert response ranging from "strongly disagree" to "strongly agree", where the high composite reliability of 0.875 is shown. In addition, the context of the research of Li et al. (2013) has been conducted in China. Moreover, they also publish the five scale items in a reputable and refereed Chinese journal (Li et al. 2012), which can help this study to ensure a more accurate translation.

Table 4.9   Measures of social decision-making constraints

Item Label	Adopted Measures	Original Measures
SDMCC1	When making a decision, I need to be concerned about how it benefits the colleague.	When making a decision, I need to be concerned about other members' benefit.
SDMCS1	When making a decision, I need to be concerned about how it benefits the superior.	
SDMCC2	It is impossible to make decisions completely according to my own preferences because I have to consider the colleague.	It is impossible to make decisions completely according to my own mind.
SDMCS2	It is impossible to make decisions completely according to my own preferences because I have to consider the superior.	
SDMCC3	The relationship with the colleague constrains my freedom in making decisions related to work.	My network constrains my freedom of making decisions.
SDMCS3	The relationship with the superior constrains my freedom in making decisions related to work.	
SDMCC4	It is imperative to consider the colleague's concerns when making decisions.	It is imperative to consider other member's concerns when making decisions.
SDMCS4	It is imperative to consider the superior's concerns when making decisions.	
SDMCC5	I have to give up my initial decisions due to "renqing" issues with the colleague.	To offer favour to my network members, I have to give up my initial decision.
SDMCS5	I have to give up my initial decisions due to "renqing" issues with the superior.	
Note	Original measures are adopted from Li et al. (2013)	

In particular, in relation to the item "to offer favour to my network members, I have to give up my initial decision", the phrase "offer favour" is the direct translation from the Chinese word "renqing", which is an important element in maintaining relationships in society in China. Simply, "renqing" can be interpreted as follows: if an individual received a favour from someone, it is expected he will return the favour to the other person. In other words, "renqing" can be interpreted as a resource that an individual can send to another individual as a gift in the course of social interaction (Hwang 1987). It means the social norms by which individuals have to abide in order to get along well with others (Gabrenya

Jr and Hwang 1996). Therefore, instead of adopting "offer favour", this study directly uses "renqing" in the fifth item.

4. 4. 7   Power distance

For the purpose of this study, power distance at the individual-level can be defined as the extent to which an individual accepts the fact that power in the institutions and organizations is distributed unequally (Clugston et al. 2000). In addition, this study establishes China as the research context: in contrast to previous studies that use Hofstede's (2001) cultural framework directly to categorise China as a high power distance, this study assesses power distance with eight items at the individual-level, taken from Kirkman et al. (2009).

Table 4. 10   Measures of power distance

Item Label	Measures from Kirkman et al. (2009)
PD1	In most situations, superiors should make decisions without consulting their subordinates.
PD2	In work-related matters, superiors have a right to expect obedience from their subordinates.
PD3	Employees who often question authority sometimes keep their superiors from being effective.
PD4	Once a superior makes a decision, subordinates should not question it.
PD5	Employees should not express disagreements with their superiors.
PD6	Superiors should be able to make the right decisions without consulting with others.
PD7	Superiors who let their subordinates participate in decisions may lose power.
PD8	A company's rules should not be broken—not even when the employee thinks it is in the company's best interest.
Note	All items are adopted from Kirkman et al. (2009) without modifications.

4. 4. 8   High-low context

Similar to the construct of power distance, rather than directly employing Hall's (1976) framework to categorise China as a high context communication style country, the construct of high-low context is measured at the individual-level. High-low context refers to the extent of non-verbal context used in communication. Warner-Søderholm (2013) develops four items to measure high-low context at the individual-level in a business setting by conducting in-depth interviews with business people, reporting a Cronbach's alpha of 0. 734. Furthermore, the scale follows the seven-point Likert-type scale with anchors of strongly disagree to strongly agree. Due to the similarity and relevance of the research level and settings, the current research adopts these measures. In addition, HLC1 and HLC3 capture the low context, while HLC2 and HLC4 capture the high context. Thus, as HLC1 and HLC3 are reverse-scored items, the item labels are changed into HLC1(R) and HLC3(R), respectively. During the data organizing, these two items are re-coded and transferred to HLC1 and HLC3 before data analysis.

Table 4. 11   Measures of high-low context

Item Label	Measures from Warner-Søderholm (2013)
HLC1(R)	Honesty is valued in meetings and discussions.
HLC2	I usually try to avoid showing disagreement openly in a discussion because we prefer to maintain a sense of harmony in meetings.
HLC3(R)	I like to "say it as it is".
HLC4	I believe that maintaining harmony and a positive tone in a meeting is more important than speaking honestly.
Note	All items are adopted from Warner-Søderholm (2013) without modifications.

4. 5   Survey layout

A survey is the most frequently used method to collect data, owing to its effectiveness in terms of gathering large empirical data (McClelland 1994). In this study, the survey has been designed to be as easy and clear to answer as possible. The full version of the survey is contained in Appendix 1. The survey is divided into two parts. Survey A aims to collect data about firm innovation, which has been completed by top managers of each firm. Survey B aims to collect data about individuals' relationships with their colleagues and superiors, which has been completed by employees.

Survey A comprises two parts:

− a cover letter, which explains the purpose and content of the survey and issues of confidentiality, as well as providing the researcher's contact details;

− the main body of Survey A, which comprises four questions, each of which involves specific sub-questions.

Survey B comprises four parts:

− a cover letter, which explains the purpose and content of the survey and issues of confidentiality, as well as providing the researcher's contact details;

− the first section of the main body of Survey B includes four questions asking respondents about their general information;

- the second section of the main body of Survey B contains 38 questions asking respondents questions regarding relationships with their superiors and colleagues;

- the final section of the main body of Survey B includes 12 questions, asking respondents about their attitudes.

Questions in Survey A reflect the dependent variable, namely the firm's innovation. These questions ask respondents to provide specific numbers about every type of innovation. Questions in Survey B reflect the underlying constructs of the conceptual model, which are presented in this instrument utilizing a seven-point Likert response ranging from "1 = strongly disagree" to "7 = strongly agree", with the exceptions of the construct of tie strength, which is presented on scales ranging from "1 = daily" to "7 = once every three months, less frequently or never" and "1 = distant" to "7 = very close".

4. 6   Translation-back-translation

Given that the survey has been developed in English but implemented in China, it needs to be translated into Chinese. This procedure is important because cultural differences may result in non-equivalence, which can confound the results (Brislin 1970; Temple 1997; Salciuviene et al. 2005). Following the experience of prior research (e. g. , Zhou et al. 2014), a translation-back-translation procedure has been undertaken (Figure 4. 2).

As can be seen in Figure 4. 2, the following steps were conducted to translate the current instrument. Firstly, the original English version was translated into Chinese and subsequently a back translation by two independent translators was commissioned. Both of the translators are native Chinese speakers with a master's degree in English, and both have experience of studying in English-speaking countries. Subsequently, the new and original English versions were compared by a small group of English-speaking researchers to ensure conceptual equivalence. If two English versions were consistent in meaning, the translation of the Chinese was successful; otherwise, the diverting items needed to be modified. Accordingly, such items needed to be back translated into English again and compared with the original English version to ensure consistency in meaning.

Since the items of the original English survey are quite simple in this study, most items were consistent in meaning after the first round of the translation-back-translation. Only two items, in terms of TR1 and SDMC5, were modified for the second round of the translation-back-translation.

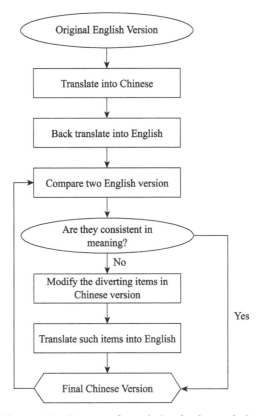

Figure 4.2   Process of translation-back-translation

4.7   Instrument refinement

According to Creswell (1994, p. 121), face validity refers to "whether items appear to measure what the instrument purports to measure", while content validity refers to "whether items measure the content they were intended to measure". In order to ensure face validity and content validity, a pre-test needed to be conducted. As none of the measures are newly developed for this research, a large scale pre-test could not be carried out. Nevertheless, face to face pilot interviews were conducted with expert academics (professors from universities in Ireland and China) and practitioners (top managers in Chinese firms). The procedures used in the pre-test are as follows.

Firstly, prior to the translation-back-translation process, the English version of the survey was reviewed by two academics (the researcher's supervisors) in Ireland regarding the feasibility of the survey. The two academics were asked to evaluate the survey to assess the relevance of its conceptualizations, refine the wording of some questions and appraise the layout the survey, which helped the researcher to arrive at the final English version of the survey.

After the translation-back-translation process, the researcher went back to China to conduct in-depth face to face interviews with two professors in China's Tianjin University and three top managers of three target high-technology firms in TEDA. After the three top managers had reviewed the survey, in-person interviews were conducted to gain their opinion on the comprehension, feasibility and relevance of items with respect to various constructs, as well as the modification of the wording of the Chinese version of the survey. 15 employees from the three firms (five employees in each firm) responded to Survey B about their working relationships with their colleagues and superiors.

Based upon the three pre-test procedures outlined above, minor changes in statement wording and layout were made to the instrument to ensure face validity and content validity. The English versions of the survey are provided in Appendix 1.

4. 8   Survey execution

As previously mentioned, snowball sampling and key informant methods have been adopted in this research. The three firms from the pre-test served as the starting point. The key informant method was adopted, whereby one top manager would represent the corresponding firm. They were asked to: 1) answer Survey A about the firm's innovation performance; 2) help to deliver Survey B to their employees; and 3) introduce the researcher to top managers they knew in other high-technology firms in TEDA or pass on the survey to high-technology firms they knew.

Table 4. 12   Number of usable surveys

	Received surveys	Usable surveys	Percentage (%)
Survey A	103	102	99. 03
Survey B	1036	1007	97. 20

The survey was conducted from November 2014 to April 2015. As indicated in Table 4. 12, 103 completed versions of Survey A were received, of which 102 were usable. 1,036 completed versions of Survey B were received, of which 1,007 were usable. The remainder were discarded, as being incompletely completed or having clear contradictions. For example, in one returned Survey B, all questions were answered by selecting the one same option only.

4. 9   Summary

This chapter introduces the research methodology undertaken in this study to answer the research questions in Chapter 1 and test the conceptual model proposed in Chapter 3. Figure 4. 3 summarizes the procedures, identifying the sections of this chapter relating to each step.

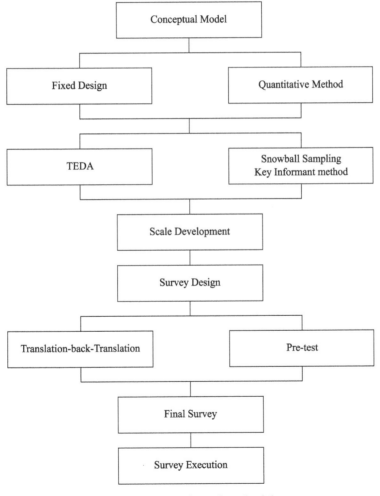

Figure 4. 3   Overview of methodology

A fixed design study has been chosen as the main research strategy. A quantitative method using a self-administered survey has been adopted to collect data about the underlying constructs proposed in the conceptual model. The current research has adopted snowball sampling and the key informant method to collect data from high-technology firms in China's TEDA.

In terms of scale development, this research has largely adopted the existing scales from prior published studies, with necessary modifications made to the original items to render them suitable to the context of the current research. The instrument used to collect the data is divided into Survey A and Survey B, relating to firms' innovation performance and employees' working relationships with their colleagues and superiors, respectively.

Given that the survey is developed in English, a translation-back-translation process is followed to derive a consistent Chinese version of the survey. A small scale pre-test has been conducted with academics and practitioners to ensure the face validity and content validity of the survey. Overall, the survey has been successfully conducted with 102 usable responses to Survey A and 1, 007 usable responses to Survey B. The next chapter details the statistical analysis undertaken, whilst accounting for the conceptual model and the nature of the data itself. In addition, the results of the hypotheses outlined earlier in Chapter 3 are presented in the chapter that follows.

Chapter 5

Data Analysis

5. 1   Introduction

   This chapter details the strategy of the statistical analysis, which takes account of the conceptual model and the nature of the data itself, and presents the results of the data analysis. Specifically, following the introduction, Section 5. 2 details the analytical method, explaining why multilevel structural equation modelling (MSEM) is used to analyse the data and how it is incorporated into the current research. Moreover, in terms of analysis strategy, Section 5. 2 also explains the two stages of the statistical analysis: the measurement model with multilevel confirmatory factor analysis (MCFA) and the multilevel structural equation model. Following on from this, Section 5. 3 presents the demographic characteristics of the data and the process of data preparation, as well as the test of normality. In relation to the two stages of the multilevel structural equation modelling process, stage-one aims to evaluate the measurement model with MCFA. Section 5. 4 provides the criteria in terms of the model fit indices of the measurement model, whilst the results from MCFA are presented in Section 5. 5. Following the establishment of the best-fitting measurement model with the refined scales from MCFA, the analysis progresses to stage-two in terms of MSEM. The results from MSEM are presented in Section 5. 6. Subsequently, the results of the moderating effects are presented in Section 5. 7. Finally, Section 5. 8 summarizes the chapter.

5. 2   Analytical method and analysis strategy

   As described in Chapter 3, this research aims to test the conceptual model

developed based on previous studies (Figure 5.1). The model proposes that social capital has various effects on social decision-making constraints, which in turn
has negative effects on firm innovation performance.

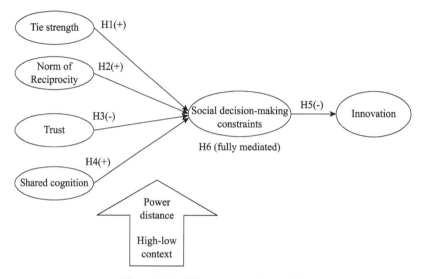

Figure 5.1   The conceptual model

This study asks individuals about their relationships with supervisors and colleagues to measure the constructs of social capital and social decision-making constraints. Therefore, the construct of social decision-making constraints and each
construct of social capital, in terms of tie strength, shared cognition, trust and
norm of reciprocity are 2nd order constructs, in that supervisor- and colleague-re-
sponses (1st order factors) reflect these constructs. The specification for the 2nd order model is presented in Figure 5.2. In this model, tie strength (TS), norm of
reciprocity (NR), trust (TR), shared cognition (SC) and social decision-making constraints (SDMC) act as the 2nd order factors. Each 2nd order factor comprises two 1st order factors.

Table 5.1   The 1st and 2nd order factors in the model

2nd order factor	1st order factor	
	Colleague-response	Supervisor-response
Tie strength (TS)	TSC	TSS
Norm of reciprocity (NR)	NRC	NRS
Trust (TR)	TRC	TRS
Shared cognition (SC)	SCC	SCS
Social decision-making constraints(SDMC)	SDMCC	SDMCS

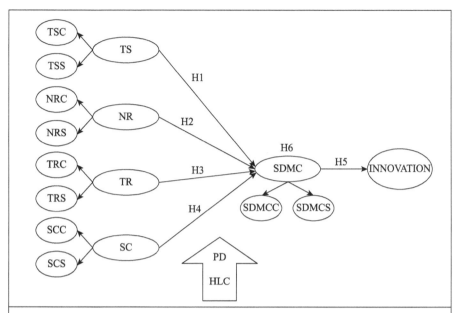

Note: TS = tie strength. NR=norm of reciprocity, TR = trust, SC = shared cognition, SDMC = social decision-making constraints, PD= power distance, HLC = high-low context. TSC. NRC.TRC, SCC, SDMCC are the colleague-response about tie strength, norm of reciprocity, trust. shared cognition and social decision-making constraints. TSS, NRS, TRS, SCS, SDMCS are the supervisor-response about tie strength, norm of reciprocity, trust, shared cognition and social decision-making constraints.

Figure 5. 2   The Model with the 2nd order factors

In order to test the model, a clear plan of the analytical process is necessary to lead the analysis in a consistent manner and to ensure the quality of the results. Therefore, in this section, the methods and strategy of the model testing are discussed.

5. 2. 1   Analytical method

Structural equation modelling (SEM), as a multivariate statistical method, has been adopted by researchers in various areas. There are four main advantages of SEM (Hair et al. 2006; Preacher et al. 2010; Stapleton 2013):

－SEM can handle a series of dependence relationships simultaneously;

－SEM enables the examination of latent variables, which are not observable and measurable directly, yet are rather inferred from at least two indicators that are directly measured;

－SEM can take account of measurement errors of observed variables;

- SEM can generate the best-fitted model by comparing the alternative models.

The current study considers SEM as the most suitable analytical method for the following reasons. Firstly, as indicated in Chapter 4, all the constructs in the conceptual model are represented latent variables which have several indicators to be measured. Secondly, SEM can take measurement error into consideration, which is unavoidable in this study due to the use of self-response indicators. Thirdly, the conceptual model includes multiple causal relationships between constructs. SEM is able to test such multiple relationships and provides test statistics for evaluating the relationships.

Specifically, the general process of SEM consists of two parts, the measurement model and the structural equation model. Before the analysis of the structural equation model (which specifies the causal relationships among constructs), it is necessary to deal with the measurement model, that is, "the relationship between observed measures or indicators and latent variables or factors" (Brown 2015, p. 1).

Confirmatory Factor Analysis (CFA) is one type of structural equation modelling that deals specifically with measurement models. The word "confirmatory" in CFA indicates that CFA is used to confirm that indicators are consistently measuring the corresponding latent variables that are pre-specified based on existing hypotheses. Therefore, the hypothesis-driven nature is the fundamental feature of CFA. Exploratory Factor Analysis (EFA), as the counterpart of CFA, focuses on exploring the pattern of relationships or underlying dimensionality among variables, where no pre-specified structures need to be determined.

In this study, each underlying latent construct (including tie strength, shared cognition, trust, norm of reciprocity, social decision-making constraints, power distance and high-low context) has been indicated by a number of observed variables. Given that all the proposed relationships between latent variables and observed indicators have been determined by the existing literature, following CFA, the theory driven approach, is more reasonable.

However, regular single-level SEM and CFA assume that cases are statistically independent. Yet, the hierarchical structure of the data violates the assumption of independence. The violation of independence can bias standard errors and lead to less accurate estimates and can affect the power of statistical significance tests (Bryk and Raudenbush 1992; Dyer et al. 2005). Moreover, according to Barbour and Lammers (2015), ignoring the nested structure of the data is conceptually and analytically problematic, given that using single-level methods with multi-level data can inadequately assume that firm-level constructs are meaningful at the individual-level or the relationship between two constructs at the individual-level apply at the firm-level.

This study aims to explore the effects of social capital at both the individual- and firm-level on innovation performance at the firm-level. As shown in Figure 5.1, the dependent variable, in terms of firm innovation performance is measured and operated at the firm-level. Whereas, the independent variables in terms of the constructs of social capital are measured at the individual-level and hypothesized to exist at both the individual-level and firm-level as the contextual constructs, the same as the mediating variables in terms of social decision-making constraints. Therefore, the model is operated at two levels.

Furthermore, the data in this study are hierarchical structure data—1,007 employees are categorized into 102 firms. That is to say, for example, if 10 employees are clustered into a firm, all these 10 employees have the same innovation performance as they are within the one firm. Therefore, it is difficult to argue that there are independent observations when employees within the firm are demonstrating the same innovation performance.

Given that the regular single-level SEM assumes that data are statistically independent, indicating its inappropriateness for the current research, this study adopts multilevel SEM (MSEM) as the specific analytical method to test the measurement model. MSEM is an advanced SEM technique developed for multilevel research by simultaneously combining SEM and multilevel modelling (Ryu 2014). Specifically, this study adopts MSEM for the following reasons.

Firstly, MSEM appropriately accounts for the hierarchical data structure that causes dependencies in the data. It is important to take the hierarchical structure of clustered data into account, given that violating the assumption of independence can underestimate the standard errors of the parameters (Cohen et al. 2013; Kelloway 2014).

Secondly, MSEM allows for an investigation of the relationship between variables at different levels in the hierarchical structure (Geiser 2012; Ryu 2014).

Thirdly, using MSEM, constructs can be measured at the individual-level and then allowed to vary at both the individual- and firm-level of analysis. The traditional method has relied on the agreement-based aggregation to measure firm-level perceptual phenomena based on individual-level responses. The firm-level variable is calculated as the average individual-level responses when quantitative agreement among members in the group reaches a certain threshold, assuming that the mathematical average of individuals' responses is a perfect indicator of the firm-level perception (Chan 1998; Cho and Dansereau 2010). This is problematic when not all individuals of a firm have provided individual-level responses and when there is not perfect agreement among individuals (Lüdtke et al. 2006). Comparing the agreement-based aggregation method that assumes that the mathematical average of individuals' responses is a perfect indicator of the firm-level perception, MSEM infers the firm-level construct from the shared variance in observed individual-level responses, which accounts for the error involved in this cross-level inference, acknowledging that the individual-levels are imperfect indicators of the firm-level perception (Kiersch 2012).

Fourthly, comparing the traditional multilevel modelling (MLM), which does not permit mediation pathways with higher level outcomes (e. g. the firm-level in the current study), MSEM does not require the outcome variables to be measured at a lower level (e. g. the individual-level in the current study) (Preacher 2010).

Additionally, prior to testing the intended proposed model of multilevel effects with MSEM, it is necessary to test the intended measurement model. Yet, the regular CFA ignores the fact that the variation can be explained in part by the nesting of the employees in the firm. In relation to the data set of this research, employees are nested with firms; multilevel confirmatory factor analysis (MCFA) is fitting. As an MSEM technique, MCFA was originally devised to test the factor structure of responses to a measurement instrument used in a study in which participants can be categorized into different groups. For example, in the current study, 1,007 participants are categorized into 102 firms. In other words, the overall relationships in the data comprise of distinct models at the individual-level of analysis and the firm-level of analysis. MCFA, indeed, aims to describe the combination of one separate factor analysis model which accounts for the structure of observations on an individual within a group, and another factor analysis model which accounts for the structure of observed groups (Klangphahol et al. 2010). Therefore, for all of the reasons outlined above, MCFA is appropriate for the purpose of the current study to evaluate the pre-specified measurement model.

Thus, in summary, due to the existence of nested or hierarchical data, this study adopts MCFA and MSEM as the analytical methods to test the measurement model and multilevel effects of the proposed model.

To perform the analysis of MSEM and MCFA, a wide variety of computer programs have been developed. The most popular computer programs include LISREL, EQS and Mplus. Each computer program has its own strengths and weaknesses. In this research, Mplus is used for model evaluation (Muthén and Muthén 2012). Mplus was developed on the basis of the computer program LIS-COMP (Muthén 1988). While retaining most features of SEM in respect of categorical and continuous data, Mplus comes with some important additions. It allows SEM models with all different types of outcome measures. Mplus enables the researcher to use all the data, with no requirement to create responses for the missing data that can alter the results. Moreover, advanced models in terms of MSEM can be readily implemented in Mplus. In addition, according to Wang and Wang (2012), the ease of use and high speed of upgrading are two of the most important advantages of Mplus. Overall, Mplus version 7. 0 is a user-friendly program that is becoming increasingly popular in SEM.

5. 2. 2　The two-stage analysis

As indicated above, the process of SEM consists of two stages, the evaluation of measurement model and structural equation modelling. In relation to the measurement model, it specifies how constructs are measured in terms of each item, and describes the measurement properties of the items. In respect of the structural equation modelling, it specifies the causal relationships among constructs and describes the amount of unexplained variance (Anderson and Gerbing 1988). The purpose of the two stages is to validate the measurement model in the first stage and fit the structural equation model in the second stage. In other words, the measurement model needs to be improved with better estimates of structural parameters and higher overall goodness of fit for use in the later stage of structural model fitting (Medsker et al. 1994).

Due to the hierarchical structure of the data in the current research, MSEM has been applied. Similar to SEM, MSEM also has a two-stage strategy in terms of the measurement model with multilevel confirmatory factor analysis and multilevel structural equation modelling. As shown in Figure 5. 3, in terms of the two-stages of the process, the analysis has been started from the model specification. The model is specified based on the conceptual model developed in Chapter 3 (see Figure 5. 1). At the same time, data preparation is carried out. Given that the assumption of normality is required for model estimation methods, the normality of data is examined. Furthermore, MCFA is carried out to test the factor structure of responses to a measurement instrument used in a study where participants can be categorized into different groups. In relation to the stage-one of MCFA, three steps are involved: (1) performing conventional CFA; (2) estimating intra-class correlation calculation; and (3) performing the MCFA.

With the refined scales from MCFA, the analysis is paved into the stage-two, in terms of MSEM. In the MSEM application, within-level and between-level are the MSEM terminologies, indicating the effects at the individual-level and firm-level, respectively. This study applies the step-wise approach of MSEM from Stapleton (2013), involving the following steps: (1) calculating the descriptive information of all variables; (2) analysing the baseline models for both within- and between-levels; (3) analysing the theoretical model at the within-level, saturated at the between-level; (4) analysing the theoretical model at the between-level, saturated at the within-level; and (5) analysing the model with the theory imposed at both levels.

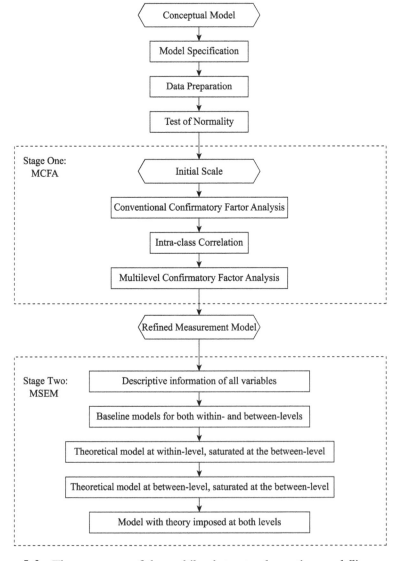

Figure 5. 3   The two-stages of the multilevel structural equation modelling process

The justification for the adoption of the step-wise approach is as follows. The applications of MSEM not only address the issue about testing and estimating the parameters in the hypothesized model, but also address the evaluation of the goodness of fit of the hypothesized model for the data, which assess how well a hypothesized model approximates the multivariate structure underlying the set of variables. Moreover, in a poor fitting model, relationships between variables cannot be reasonably interpreted, given that a poor fitting model does not approximate the underlying structure observed in the data (Ryu 2014). Therefore, instead of analysing the multilevel model directly, this study applies the step-wise approach from Stapleton (2013).

The first step provides statistical evidence about whether the multilevel analysis is appropriate for the data. Step 2 provides initial information about the model fit indices of the within-and between-level independence model. Steps 3 and 4 separately provide the model fit indices of hypothesized relationships at the within- and between-level of the multilevel model. If the fit is poor, the evaluation of the within- or between-level theory should be conducted to improve the model fit. Also, when the final step results in a poor model fit, the results of these steps provide information about whether the model fit is poor at the within-level, at the between-level, or at both levels. Therefore, before the final step, in terms of the actual MSEM that simultaneously evaluates the proposed model at both levels, it is necessary and significant to conduct the first four steps. This is because such steps can provide the pertinent information used to justify the adoption of multilevel analysis and initial information about the fit indices at different levels of analysis, which can provide useful information for setting starting values for the estimation of the MSEM if it fails to converge.

5.3   Data Characteristics and Preparation

Before using the data for further analysis, it is necessary to organise the original data set. Section 5.3.1 provides a demographic analysis of the responses. Section 5.3.2 details the treatment of reverse coded items. Finally, the normality of the data for each item has been tested in Section 5.3.3, which is necessary to choose the method of estimation.

5.3.1   Demographic characteristics

This section provides a demographic analysis of the 1,007 responses in 102 firms. Results of participants' ages, education, experience of working or studying abroad and the sectors of the responding firms are presented in Table 5. 2 to 5. 7.

Table 5. 2 reveals that the 40. 6 percent of respondents are aged between 29–35 years old, 27. 6 percent are aged between 36–42 years old, and 21. 3 percent are aged between 23-28 years old. Therefore, the majority of respondents (89. 5 percent) fall into the 23–42 years old category. In Table 5. 3, results reveal that most of the participants have classified their highest level of degree achievement as a bachelor's degree (53. 5 percent), followed by a master's degree qualification (31. 8 percent).

Table 5. 2   Age of respondent

Age	Frequency	Percent (%)
18-22	1	0. 1
23-28	214	21. 3
29-35	409	40. 6
36-42	278	27. 6
43-50	91	9. 0
50-60	14	1. 4
over 60	0	0
Total	1007	100

Table 5. 3   Education of respondent

Education	Frequency	Percent (%)
High school	87	8. 6
Bachelor's degree	539	53. 5
Master's degree	320	31. 8
Doctor's degree	61	6. 1
Total	1007	100

As shown in Table 5. 4, the majority of respondents (87. 2 percent) do not have any experience of either studying or working abroad for a period more than one year. Among the 12. 8 percent of respondents who report to have either studied or worked abroad for more than one year, almost half (49. 6 percent) of them have studied or worked in the United States (21. 7 percent), followed by Australia (17. 1 percent) and UK (10. 8 percent). Moreover, the majority of respondents (66. 7 percent) have spent 12-23 months either studying or working abroad (Table 5. 4 to 5. 6).

Table 5. 4   Experience of studying or working abroad

Abroad	Frequency	Percent (%)
Yes	129	12. 8
No	878	87. 2
Total	1,007	100

Table 5. 5   Country

Country	Frequency	Valid Percent (%)	Percent (%)
Australia	22	17. 1	2. 2
Belgium	1	0. 8	0. 1
Canada	10	7. 8	1
Denmark	2	1. 6	0. 2
Finland	1	0. 8	0. 1
France	4	3. 0	0. 4
Germany	9	7. 0	0. 9
Hong Kong, China	11	8. 5	1. 1
Ireland	2	1. 6	0. 2
Italy	4	3. 0	0. 4
Japan	5	3. 9	0. 5
Netherlands	2	1. 6	0. 2
New Zealand	3	2. 3	0. 3
Singapore	3	2. 3	0. 3
South Africa	1	0. 8	0. 1
South Korea	3	2. 3	0. 3
Spain	2	1. 6	0. 2
Sweden	1	0. 8	0. 1
Taiwan, China	1	0. 8	0. 1
UK	14	10. 8	1. 4
US	28	21. 7	2. 8
Total	129	100	12. 8
No abroad experience	878		87. 2
Total	1,007		100

Table 5. 6   Period of studying or working abroad

Period (months)	Frequency	Valid Percent (%)	Percent (%)
12-23	86	66. 7	8. 5
24-35	14	10. 9	1. 4
36-47	7	5. 4	0. 7
More than 48	22	17. 1	2. 2
Total	129	100	12. 8
No experience of either studying or working abroad	878		87. 2
Total	1, 007		100

The sample consists of 17 high-technology firms and 85 small and medium scientific and technology firms (Table 5. 7). TEDA lists all firms of various categorizations on its official website (Miller and Breton-Miller 2006). This secondary data was used to categorize the sample firms.

Table 5. 7   Category of participating firms

Category	Frequency	Percent (%)
High-technology firm	17	16. 7
Small and medium scientific and technology firm	85	83. 3
Total	102	100

As shown in Table 5. 8, responding firms cover 6 high-technology sectors. Typical responding sectors include manufacture of machinery and equipment and telecommunications (54. 9 percent).

Table 5. 8   Sector

Sector (NACE code)	Frequency	Percent (%)
Telecommunications (61)	25	24. 5
Manufacture of motor vehicles, trailers and semi-trailers (29)	16	15. 7
Manufacture of machinery and equipment (28)	31	30. 4
Manufacture of electrical equipment (27)	11	10. 8
Manufacture of chemicals and chemical products (20)	11	10. 8
Manufacture of basic pharmaceutical products and pharmaceutical preparations (21)	8	7. 8
Total	102	100

Table 5. 9   Number of Survey B's returned by participating firms

Number of Survey B	Frequency	Percent (%)
5	3	2. 9
6	5	4. 9
7	9	8. 8
8	15	14. 7
9	13	12. 7
10	24	23. 5
11	12	11. 8
12	10	9. 8
13	5	4. 9
15	2	2. 0
16	1	1. 0
17	1	1. 0
19	1	1. 0
23	1	1. 0
Total	1, 007	102	100
Min	5		
Max	23		
Average	10		

In addition, the average number of Survey B's returned by participating firms is 10. As presented in Table 5. 9, for example, the first line in the table reveals that each of the three firms returned five survey Bs. There are 72. 5 percent of participating firms who returned eight to twelve Survey B's.

Table 5. 10   Descriptive results of firm's innovation performance

Innovation		Min	Max	Mean	Std. Deviation
Product		3	51	17. 09	9. 62
	New to the world	0	8	1. 75	2. 06
	New to the firm	1	18	5. 11	3. 66
	Major changes	0	13	5. 07	3. 05
	Minor changes	0	13	4. 95	2. 61
Process		3	50	17. 03	11. 44
Marketing		3	36	14. 61	8. 02
Organizational		4	56	21. 90	11. 33

Regarding the firm's innovation performance, the average numbers of product (17. 09), process (17. 03), marketing (14. 61) and organizational (21. 90) innovation in participating firms are presented in Table 5. 10. Regarding the maximum number of each type of innovation, the largest category is the number of organizational innovation (56), while the smallest category is the number of new to the world product innovation (8).

5. 3. 2   Reverse coded items

Among all the survey items, there are reverse coded items, in terms of TS2C(R), TS2S(R), HLC1(R) and HLC3(R), which need to be recoded so that they can have a consistent pattern with the rest of the items in the same construct. Under the construct of tie strength, TS2C(R) and TS2S(R) are reverse coded, because all the items under this construct measure the closeness and frequency of the relationship; TS1C and TS1S are positively related to the level of closeness (ranging from "1 = very distant" to "7 = very close"). However, TS2C (R) and TS2S(R) are negatively related to the extent of communication frequency (ranging from "1 = daily" to "7 = once every three months, less frequently or never"). Therefore, TS2C(R) and TS2S(R) need to be recoded to TS2C and TS2S by "8-x", that is: 1 becomes 7; 2 becomes 6; 3 becomes 5; 4 becomes 4; 5 becomes 3; 6 becomes 2; and 7 becomes 1.

In the same vein, HLC1(R) and HLC3(R) are also reverse coded items. HLC2 and HLC4 are associated with high context, whereas, HLC1 (R) and HLC3(R) are related to low context. Thus, HLC1(R) and HLC3(R) need to be transformed into HLC1 and HLC3 employing the same method as specified above.

5. 3. 3   Test of normality

Data normality for each item needs to be checked by determining the skewness and kurtosis statistics, which are the evidence used to decide on the estimation method. For instance, it is worth noting that the commonly used estimation method, in terms of Maximum Likelihood is appropriate for the data with normality assumptions. The method in terms of Robust Maximum Likelihood is suggested to generate more accurate test statistics for data that violate normality assumptions (Curran et al. 1996).

Using SPSS software to test the skewness and kurtosis, the results indicate that most variables have skewness or kurtosis in the range of -1 to +1, which indicates the presence of normality (Hair et al. 2006). The test results suggest that the commonly used Maximum Likelihood (ML) is appropriate.

The details of the results of the test of skewness and kurtosis are presented in Appendix 2 (Table A1).

5. 4　Model fit indices

With the data organizing completed, the main statistical analysis has been started with the measurement model evaluation. The purpose of the evaluation of the measurement model is to refine and validate the original scale. As indicated previously, MCFA has been used in this research as the statistical method to assess the measurement model. This section details the criteria in terms of the model fit indices to evaluate the validity of constructs.

In relation to the model fit indices, this study uses five indices (including χ^2, χ^2/df, CFI, TLI, RMSEA and SRMR) to assess the fit of the measurement model for the data with the MCFA. In multilevel analysis, the acceptable values of these fit statistics are the same as in single-level analysis (Johnson et al. 2005). Thus, according to prior studies (e. g. Hu and Bentler 1999; Schermelleh-Engel et al. 2003; Geiser 2012), the cut-off values for an acceptable fit are as follows:

$-\chi^2$, which is adjusted for normality, is used to evaluate the model fit. The ratio of χ^2/df indicates a better fit index because it is less sensitive regarding sample sizes. Kline (2010) suggests that a ratio of less than 3 can indicate a good model fit. Nevertheless, a more liberal criterion of 5 is also commonly employed (Bentler 1989).

$-$ CFI (Comparative Fit Index) is the proportion in the improvement of the overall fit of the existing model to the null model. A value greater than 0. 90 can indicate an acceptable model fit (Hu and Bentler 1999).

$-$ TLI (Tucker-Lewis Index) compares the fit of the target model to the fit of the independence model. TLI has the same cut-off values (greater than 0. 90) as those that apply to CFI (Hu and Bentler 1999).

$-$ RMSEA (Root Mean Square Error of Approximation) coefficient is a measure of approximate model fit. The values of RMSEA below 0. 05 are usually seen as indicative of a good fit (Fang 2010).

$-$ SRMR (Standardized Root Mean Square Residual) coefficient is a standardized measure for the evaluation of model residuals. A good model should have a value of SRMR smaller than 0. 08 (Hair et al. 2006).

5. 5   Results from multilevel Confirmatory Factor Analysis

The process to access the measurement model involves three steps: (1) performing conventional CFA, (2) calculating the intra-class correlation calculation, and (3) performing the MCFA. The results of each step are presented in Sections 5. 5. 1 to 5. 5. 3.

5. 5. 1   Conventional CFA

Before conducting the MCFA, this section attempts a conventional single-level CFA. As indicated above, the parameter estimates and fit statistics resulting from the single-level CFA may be biased when the degree of non-independence is substantial. However, performing the single-level CFA can suggest potential refinements. The items with lower standard factor loadings especially can lead to difficulties in fitting data (Johnson et al. 2005).

Table 5. 11 presents the fit indices for the conventional CFA, demonstrating that the single-level model fits the data. Meanwhile, when factor loadings are examined (Figure 5. 4), SCC1 SCS1 SCC2 and SCS2 are found to have small standardized factor loadings with the corresponding latent variables. In subsequent multilevel analyses, the loadings of these items are further examined (in Section 5. 5. 3). The item of TRS is set to zero in order to avoid a negative variance estimate (Muthén and Muthén 2012), which is shown in Figure 5. 4 (with a factor loading of 1. 00).

Table 5. 11   Fit indices from CFA, Model$_{single}$

CFA Model	χ^2	df	χ^2/df	CFI	TFI	RMSEA	SRMR
Model$_{single}$	1388. 60	795	1. 75	0. 96	0. 96	0. 02	0. 03

As discussed earlier, the conventional single-level CFA fails to incorporate the hierarchical nature of the data and therefore, the analysis can be potentially misleading. The results can only suggest some potential refinements, given that such results can be influenced by the firm-level factor structure when there is substantial systematic between-group variance. Thus, the next step is to assess the amount of between-group level information.

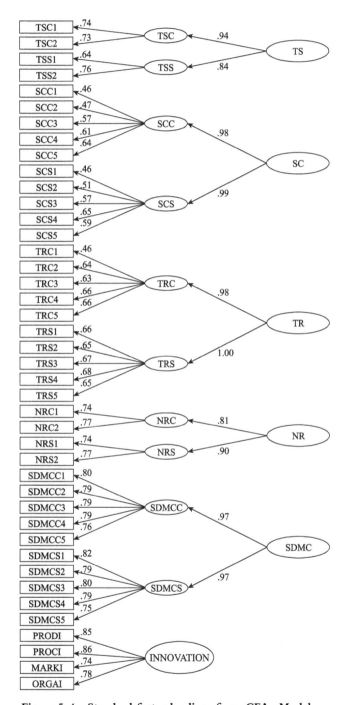

Figure 5.4   Standard factor loadings from CFA, Model$_{single}$

5. 5. 2   Intra-class correlation

Before analysing MCFA, the intra-class correlation (ICC) for each item should be calculated. The purpose of estimating the ICC is to address the question about whether the multilevel analysis is appropriate for the data (Dyer et al. 2005). The ICC is defined as a ratio of variance that exists at the firm-level (Kelloway 2014). The value of the ICC should be reviewed to determine the appropriateness of the multilevel model. In other words, ICC measures the degree of dependence of observations. The range of ICC value is from 0 to 1; an ICC of 0 indicates that the observations are independent of cluster membership. If the ICC values are close to 0, MCFA and MSEM can be very difficult, given that there is minimal between-firm variance to model and estimation convergence can be a problem (Stapleton 2013). The larger the values of ICC, the more individual differences are due to differences between clusters. In this study, ICC should be calculated for all items of every latent variable at the individual-level, in terms of every item of the constructs of tie strength, shared cognition, norm of reciprocity, trust and social decision-making constraints.

As shown in Table 5. 12, the ICC's range of each item is from 0. 16 to 0. 48, with an average ICC of 0. 33. The relatively high ICC values suggest a reasonable amount of variability to be modelled at the firm-level.

Table 5. 12   ICC values of each item

Item	Construct				
	Tie strength	Norm of reciprocity	Trust	Shared cognition	Social decision-making constraints
TS1C	0. 41				
TS2C	0. 47				
TS1S	0. 28				
TS2S	0. 35				
NR1C		0. 28			
NR2C		0. 27			
NR1S		0. 28			
NR2S		0. 20			
TR1C			0. 37		
TR2C			0. 28		

continued

Item	Construct				
	Tie strength	Norm of reciprocity	Trust	Shared cognition	Social decision-making constraints
TR3C			0. 31		
TR4C			0. 31		
TR5C			0. 30		
TR1S			0. 32		
TR2S			0. 29		
TR3S			0. 33		
TR4S			0. 32		
TR5S			0. 31		
SC1C				0. 19	
SC2C				0. 18	
SC3C				0. 27	
SC4C				0. 22	
SC5C				0. 26	
SC1S				0. 22	
SC2S				0. 26	
SC3S				0. 16	
SC4S				0. 23	
SC5S				0. 24	
SDMC1C					0. 45
SDMC2C					0. 46
SDMC3C					0. 43
SDMC4C					0. 41
SDMC5C					0. 39
SDMC1S					0. 43
SDMC2S					0. 42
SDMC3S					0. 42
SDMC4S					0. 41
SDMC5S					0. 41

Note: TS, NR, TR, SC and SDMC represent tie strength, shared cognition, trust, norm of reciprocity and social decision-making constraints, separately. TSC, NRC, TRC, SCC and SDMCC are the employee-responses about tie strength, shared cognition, trust, norm of reciprocity, and social decision-making constraints. TSS, NRS, TRS, SCS and SDMCS are the supervisor-responses about tie strength, shared cognition, trust, norm of reciprocity and social decision-making constraints.

5.5.3 Perform MCFA

The ICC values of each item justify the appropriateness of multilevel analysis. In the application of MCFA and MSEM, within-level and between-level are the terminologies, indicating the effects at individual-level and firm-level, respectively. Therefore, instead of using the term "firm-level" and "individual-level" as in Figure 3.2 (in terms of the multilevel conceptual model), at this stage of the data analysis, the terminologies of within-level and between-level are adopted (Figure 5.5).

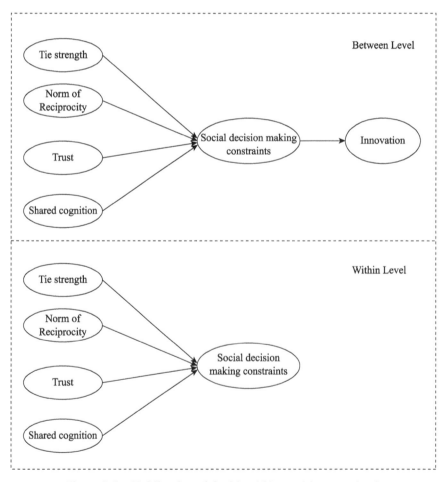

Figure 5.5   Multilevel model with within- and between-level

This section employs MCFA to simultaneously estimate the within- and between-level models (see Figure 5.5) for the purpose of incorporating the hierarchical nature of the data. Table 5.13 presents the results of the MCFA, suggesting that the CFI, TLI and $SRMR_{between}$ are somewhat below the recommended thresholds (χ^2/df = 1.62, CFI = 0.93, TLI = 0.93, RMSEA = 0.02, and $SRMR_{within}$ = 0.03, $SRMR_{between}$ = 0.10). As indicated by Johnson et al. (2005), the primary difficulty in fitting data to a model is that some of the items do not load well together. According to their study, items which failed to load well together are dropped from the constructs in order to achieve a good fit for the data. Moreover, Dyer et al. (2005) reveal that estimation problems can lead to a failure to converge. When this happens, they suggest that the parameter estimates for factor loadings from both conventional CFA and MCFA can provide the start values.

Table 5.13   Fit indices for MCFA, $Model_{multi1}$

MCFA model	χ^2	df	χ^2/df	CFI	TLI	RMSEA	SRMR	
							Within	Between
$Model_{multi1}$	2329.20	1439	1.62	0.93	0.93	0.02	0.03	0.10

Tables 5.14 and 5.15 present the standard factor loading of every item at the within- and between-level from MCFA. Overall, consistent with the belief that the constructs in this study are primarily operating at the firm-level of analysis, the items load strongly at the between-level; however, it is evident that the factor loadings of the items at the within-level are not as strong as those at the between-level.

Table 5.14   Standard factor loadings at the within-level from MCFA, $Model_{multi1}$

	Construct			
	Tie strength		Norm of reciprocity	
Item	TSC	TSS	NRC	NRS
TSC1	0.73			
TSC2	0.55			
TSS1		0.56		
TSS2		0.72		
NRC1			0.63	
NRC2			0.70	
NRS1				0.62
NRS2				0.71

Table 5. 14   Standard factor loadings at the within-level from MCFA,
Model$_{multil}$ (Continued)

Item	Trust		Shared cognition		Social decision-making constraints	
	TRC	TRS	SCC	SCS	SDMCC	SDMCS
TRC1	0. 44					
TRC2	0. 47					
TRC3	0. 47					
TRC4	0. 41					
TRC5	0. 42					
TRS1		0. 41				
TRS2		0. 46				
TRS3		0. 42				
TRS4		0. 48				
TRS5		0. 43				
SCC1			0. 45			
SCC2			0. 45			
SCC3			0. 48			
SCC4			0. 47			
SCC5			0. 46			
SCS1				0. 47		
SCS2				0. 43		
SCS3				0. 51		
SCS4				0. 52		
SCS5				0. 41		
SDMCC1					0. 64	
SDMCC2					0. 60	
SDMCC3					0. 63	
SDMCC4					0. 63	
SDMCC5					0. 59	
SDMCS1						0. 66
SDMCS2						0. 60
SDMCS3						0. 62
SDMCS4						0. 63
SDMCS5						0. 60

Table 5.15   Standard factor loadings at the between-level from MCFA,
Model$_{multi1}$

Item	Innovation	Tie strength		Norm of reciprocity		Trust	
		TSC	TSS	NRC	NRS	TRC	TRS
PRODI	0.84						
PROCI	0.88						
MARKI	0.76						
ORGAI	0.76						
TSC1		0.84					
TSC2		0.88					
TSS1			0.79				
TSS2			0.86				
NRC1				0.97			
NRC2				0.98			
NRS1					0.98		
NRS2					1.00		
TRC1						0.93	
TRC2						0.99	
TRC3						0.90	
TRC4						0.99	
TRC5						0.99	
TRS1							0.99
TRS2							0.98
TRS3							0.98
TRS4							0.98
TRS5							0.99

Table 5. 15   Standard factor loadings at the between-level from MCFA,
Model$_{multi1}$ (Continued)

| Item | Construct | | | |
| | Shared cognition | | Social decision-making constraints | |
	SCC	SCS	SDMCC	SDMCS
SCC1	0. 55			
SCC2	0. 64			
SCC3	0. 80			
SCC4	0. 96			
SCC5	0. 99			
SCS1		0. 50		
SCS2		0. 73		
SCS3		0. 93		
SCS4		0. 99		
SCS5		0. 99		
SDMCC1			0. 96	
SDMCC2			0. 98	
SDMCC3			0. 98	
SDMCC4			0. 98	
SDMCC5			0. 96	
SDMCS1				0. 99
SDMCS2				0. 98
SDMCS3				0. 99
SDMCS4				0. 99
SDMCS5				0. 93

From the single-level CFA in Section 5.5.1, the items, in terms of SCC1 SCC2 SCS1 and SCS2 do not load well (see Figure 5.4). Similar to the result from single-level CFA, SCC1 SCC2 SCS1 and SCS2 are found to have small factor loadings with the corresponding latent variables at the within- and between-level from MCFA. SCC1 and SCS1 refer to the questions of "The colleague and I use understandable language to communicate with each other" and "The superior and I use understandable language to communicate with each other". SCC2 and SCS2 refer to the questions of "The colleague and I prefer to use the same means to communicate with each other" and "The superior and I prefer to use the same means of communication with each other". All the four items aim to measure one of the major manifestations of shared cognition, in terms of shared language.

Given that using understandable language to communicate with colleagues and superiors is the most basic skill when individuals work together, 83.1 percent of respondents in this study (the sum of percentages who answer this question by choosing 5-7, that is the sum of 24.0, 37.6 and 21.5 percents) believe that they can use understandable language to communicate with their colleagues and superiors. Moreover, in relation to the means to communicate, such as face to face, text or Email, the majority of respondents were satisfied about that the way they communicate with their colleagues (75.4 percent) and superiors (57 percent) (see Table 5.16 for details). Such percentages above indicate that there is little variance in the responses to these questions, which negatively impacts the factor loadings.

Table 5.16   Descriptive statistics of SCC1 SCS1 SCC2 and SCS2

Items / Responses		SCC1	SCS1	SCC2	SCS2
		Percentage (%)			
Strongly disagree	1	3.6	3.4	3.7	5.3
	2	2.3	2.9	3.9	6.6
	3	3.2	3.1	4.6	10.9
	4	7.8	7.5	12.5	20.3
	5	23.3	24.0	24.7	32.7
Strongly agree	6	36.0	37.6	31.4	12.2
	7	23.8	21.5	19.3	12.1

From the theoretical perspective, in addition to shared language, the importance of another major manifestation of shared cognition, in terms of shared vision is highlighted. Shared language can lead to less misunderstanding. Nevertheless, common goals and interests not only can help employees to avoid misunderstandings, overlapping with the role of shared language, but also provide more opportunities to increase the commitment to exploit synergies (Tsai and Ghoshal 1998; Villena et al. 2011). Therefore, being cognisant of both statistical and theoretical considerations, SCC1 SCS1 SCC2 and SCS2 have been deleted at both the within- and between-level in this study.

With the four items eliminated at both within- and between-levels, another MCFA is conducted ($Model_{multi2}$). The results in Table 5.17 show a significant improvement in model fit ($\chi^2/df = 1.48$, CFI = 0.95, TLI = 0.95, RMSEA = 0.02, and $SRMR_{within}$ = 0.03, $SRMR_{between}$ = 0.06), justifying that all of the model fit indices are above the acceptable level.

Table 5.17   Fit indices for MCFA, $Model_{multi1}$ and $Model_{multi2}$

MCFA model	χ^2	df	χ^2/df	CFI	TLI	RMSEA	SRMR	
							Within	Between
$Model_{multi1}$	2329.20	1439	1.62	0.93	0.93	0.02	0.03	0.10
$Model_{multi2}$	1698.41	1147	1.48	0.95	0.95	0.02	0.03	0.06

The factor loadings of $Model_{multi2}$ from MCFA are presented in Table 5.18 and 5.19. In addition, Figure 5.6 presents the factor loadings of the 2nd order factor from $Model_{multi2}$. The negative residual variances are set to zero, showing in Tables 5.18 to 5.19 and Figure 5.5 a factor loading of 1.00. The factor loadings of the 2nd order factor from $Model_{multi1}$ are not reported, given that they are very similar in value to the estimates from $Model_{multi2}$.

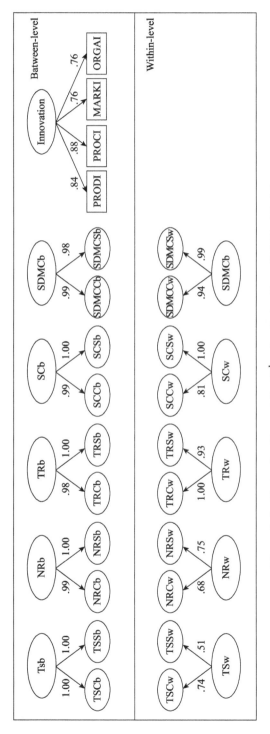

Figure 5.6   Factor loadings of the 2nd order factor from MCFA, Model$_{multi2}$

Table 5.18　　　　Standard factor loadings at the within-level from MCFA, Model$_{multi2}$

| | Construct | | | | | | | Construct | | | |
| | Tie strength | | Norm of reciprocity | | Trust | | | Shared cognition | | Social decision-making constraints | |
Item	TSC	TSS	NRC	NRS	TRC	TRS	Item	SCC	SCS	SDMCC	SDMCS
TSC1	0.74						TRC3	0.54			
TSC2	0.54						TRC4	0.48			
TSS1		0.55					TRC5	0.47			
TSS2		0.73					TRS3		0.47		
NRC1			0.63				TRS4		0.54		
NRC2			0.70				TRS5		0.38		
NRS1				0.62			SDMCC1			0.64	
NRS2				0.71			SDMCC2			0.60	
TRC1					0.44		SDMCC3			0.63	
TRC2					0.46		SDMCC4			0.63	
TRC3					0.47		SDMCC5			0.60	
TRC4					0.41		SDMCS1				0.66
TRC5					0.42		SDMCS2				0.60
TRS1						0.41	SDMCS3				0.62
TRS2						0.45	SDMCS4				0.62
TRS3						0.42	SDMCS5				0.60
TRS4						0.48					
TRS5						0.43					

Table 5.19   Standard factor loading at the between–level from MCFA, Model$_{multi2}$

Item	Construct						Item	Construct				
	Tie strength		Norm of reciprocity		Trust			Shared cognition		Social decision–making constraints		Innovation
	TSC	TSS	NRC	NRS	TRC	TRS		SCC	SCS	SDMCC	SDMCS	
TSC1	0.84						SCC3	0.78				
TSC2	0.88						SCC4	0.96				
TSS1		0.788					SCC5	1.00				
TSS2		0.857					SCS3		0.89			
NRC1			0.97				SCS4		0.99			
NRC2			0.98				SCS5		0.97			
NRS1				0.99			SDMCC1			0.96		
NRS2				1.00			SDMCC2			0.97		
TRC1					0.93		SDMCC3			0.98		
TRC2					0.99		SDMCC4			0.98		
TRC3					0.90		SDMCC5			0.96		
TRC4					0.99		SDMCS1				0.99	
TRC5					0.99		SDMCS2				0.97	
TRS1						0.99	SDMCS3				0.99	
TRS2						0.98	SDMCS4				0.99	
TRS3						0.98	SDMCS5				0.93	
TRS4						0.97	PRODI					0.84
TRS5						0.96	PROCI					0.88
							MARKI					0.76
							ORGAI					0.76

To conclude, the results from MCFA provide support for the stability of the Model$_{multi2}$. Specifically, the four constructs of social capital, as well as the construct of social decision-making constraints can be analysed with the multilevel model. The factor loading values at the within-level are less than that at the between-level, indicating that the multilevel structure of the scale confirms the expectation that the constructs in this study are primarily operating at the firm-level of analysis.

The validation of the MCFA model confirms that the Model$_{multi2}$ has structural validity and fit the empirical data well, facilitating the next stage of MSEM which tests the theoretical hypotheses at the multilevel of analysis.

5. 6   Multilevel Structural Equation Modelling (MSEM)

The MCFA procedure ensures the stability of the measurement model of Model$_{multi2}$, and paves the way for MSEM in this section. First of all, it is necessary to ensure that there is sufficient between-level variability to support MSEM. With the statistical evidence regarding the appropriateness of multilevel analysis for the data, applications of MSEM address two issues as follows: (1) assessing the goodness of fit of the hypothesized model for the data; and (2) testing the parameters in the hypothesized model. Issue (2) can only be addressed in a meaningful way when issue (1) results in a well-fitting model. If the entire multilevel model were directly evaluated and resulted in a poor model fit, it is difficult to diagnose whether the model fit is poor at the within-level, at the between-level, or at both levels. Therefore, Stapleton's (2013) step-wise approach that allows for an evaluation of the plausibility of the model at each level, has been applied in the current research.

Overall, the first step is to calculate ICC values to answer the question about whether multilevel analysis is appropriate for the data. Steps 2 to 4 separately evaluate the model fit at the within- and between-level respectively, providing valuable information in the evaluation of the final MSEM model. The final step assesses the model fit of the entire multilevel model, and tests the hypothesized relationship in the multilevel model. The results of the five steps are presented in Sections 5. 6. 1 to 5. 6. 5.

5. 6. 1   Step 1: Calculate the descriptive information of all variables

Before any analysis, it is important to inspect each of the analysis variables. In relation to the two-level analysis, a significant step is to inspect how much homogeneity exists within clusters, in terms of the ICC values of all variables. Before the MCFA, Section 5.5.2 presents the ICC values of all items. Given that items have been refined with MCFA, this section recalculates the ICC values with refined items of corresponding constructs in the $Model_{multi2}$ and presents the estimates in Table 5.20.

Compared to the ICC values of the original items in Section 5.5.2, the ICC values of the refined items are only changed slightly. The ICC values are ranging from 0.16 to 0.47, suggesting the appropriateness of multilevel modelling to address the hypotheses.

Table 5.20   ICC values of refined items of $Model_{multi2}$

Item	Construct				
	Tie strength	Norm of reciprocity	Trust	Shared cognition	Social decision-making constraints
TS1C	0.41				
TS2C	0.47				
TS1S	0.28				
TS2S	0.36				
NR1C		0.29			
NR2C		0.27			
NR1S		0.28			
NR2S		0.21			
TR1C			0.37		
TR2C			0.29		
TR3C			0.32		
TR4C			0.31		
TR5C			0.32		
TR1S			0.33		
TR2S			0.30		
TR3S			0.33		
TR4S			0.32		
TR5S			0.31		
SC3C				0.27	

continued

	Construct				
Item	Tie strength	Norm of reciprocity	Trust	Shared cognition	Social decision-making constraints
SC4C				0. 23	
SC5C				0. 26	
SC3S				0. 16	
SC4S				0. 23	
SC5S				0. 24	
SDMC1C					0. 45
SDMC2C					0. 46
SDMC3C					0. 43
SDMC4C					0. 41
SDMC5C					0. 38
SDMC1S					0. 44
SDMC2S					0. 43
SDMC3S					0. 42
SDMC4S					0. 41
SDMC5S					0. 42

5. 6. 2   Step 2: Run the baseline models for both the within- and be-tween- levels

It is necessary to review the model testing strategies before attempting to ana-lyse the theoretical model. Before analysing the partially-saturated models, where the fit of the within- and between-level model from the multilevel model is tested respectively, this step aims to provide initial information about the model fit indi-ces of the within-and between-level independence model beforehand, expecting to help to troubleshoot from simpler models before conducting the complex mul-tilevel model.

Specifically, adopting the approach of Stapleton (2013), this step involves the subsequent two baseline models, in terms of $Model_{b1}$ and $Model_{b2}$. $Modelb_1$ allows all the variables to covary at the between-level and restricts all variable co-variance values to 0 at the within-level. $Model_{b2}$ allows all variables to covary at the within-level and restricts all variable covariance values to 0 at the between-level.

This step runs the baseline models to test the plausibility of the imposed theoretical model with χ^2 test information. The baseline χ^2 value for the within-level $Model_{b1}$ is 1,928.44 with 1,157 degrees of freedom, while the baseline χ^2 value for the between-level $Model_{b2}$ is 3,703.73 with 1,162 degrees of freedom. Table 5.21 reports the fit statistics of the baseline models.

Table 5.21   Fit indices for baseline models, $Model_{b1}$ and $Model_{b2}$

Baseline model	χ^2	df	χ^2/df	CFI	TLI	RMSEA	SRMR	
							Within	Between
$Model_{b1}$	1928.44	1157	1.67	0.93	0.93	0.02	0.06	0.08
$Model_{b2}$	3703.73	1162	3.18	0.88	0.86	0.40	0.03	0.12

5.6.3   Step 3: Run the theoretical model at the within-level, saturated at the between-level

This step examines the plausibility of the within-level hypothesized relations of the multilevel model. In this analysis, all variables at the between-level are allowed to freely covary with each other, indicating the model is saturated at the between-level. Therefore, the fit indices of this model suggest whether the theory imposed at the within-level is plausible.

Table 5.22   Fit indices for the theoretical within-model of $Model_{multi2}$

Within-level model	χ^2	df	χ^2/df	CFI	TLI	RMSEA	SRMR	
							Within	Between
$Model_{within}$	1856.17	1147	1.62	0.95	0.94	0.02	0.03	0.06

As presented in Table 5.22, the χ^2 test of model fit for this model is 1,856.17 with 1,147 degrees of freedom, suggesting a good fit at the within-level. SRMR values for this model are 0.03 at the within-level and 0.06 at the between-level. As all the fit indices are acceptable at the within-level, the next step is to impose the hypothesized relations at the between-level.

5.6.4   Step 4: Run the theoretical model at the between-level, saturated at the within-level

This step runs a saturated model at the within-level (in which all variables at the within-level are allowed to freely covary) and imposes the hypothesized model at the between-level. Tests of model fit evaluate the plausibility of the between-level model (Table 5. 23). The χ^2 test of model fit for this model is 1, 701. 43 with 1, 151 degrees of freedom, suggesting a good fit at the between-level. The CFI is 0. 95, and the SRMR are 0. 03 and 0. 08, respectively. As these fit statistics indicate acceptable model fit at the between-level, the analysis can proceed to simultaneous evaluation of both levels of the model.

Table 5. 23   Fit indices for the theoretical between-model of Model$_{multi2}$

Between- level model	χ^2	df	χ^2/df	CFI	TLI	RMSEA	SRMR	
							Within	Between
Model$_{between}$	1701. 43	1151	1. 48	0. 95	0. 95	0. 02	0. 03	0. 08

5. 6. 5   Step 5: Run the model with theory imposed at both levels

Given the acceptable fit at both the within- and between-level, this step simultaneously evaluates both levels of the multilevel model in terms of Model$_{multi2}$. The illustration of the Model$_{multi2}$ is shown in Figure 5. 7.

Table 5. 24   Fit indices of the multilevel model, Model$_{multi2}$

MSEM	χ^2	df	χ^2/df	CFI	TLI	RMSEA	SRMR	
							Within	Between
Model$_{multi}$	1701. 43	1151	1. 48	0. 95	0. 95	0. 02	0. 03	0. 07

The fit indices shown in Table 5. 24 indicate that the hypothesized Model$_{multi2}$ provides a good fit for the data. The χ^2 test statistic is 1, 701. 43 with 1, 151 degrees of freedom and the SRMR values are 0. 03 and 0. 07 for the within and between-levels, respectively. As a result, the hypotheses can be evaluated via the path coefficients.

As indicated in Table 5. 25, assessment of the parameter estimates results suggest that all the paths from tie strength and trust to social decision-making constraints are statistically significant at both the within-and between-level. Yet the path from shared cognition to social decision-making constraints is not statistically significant. At the within-level, the relationship between norm of reciprocity and social decision-making constraints is positive and significant, but not significant at the between-level. At the between-level, the path from social decision-making constraints to firm innovation performance is statistically significant with the hypothesized negative relationship.

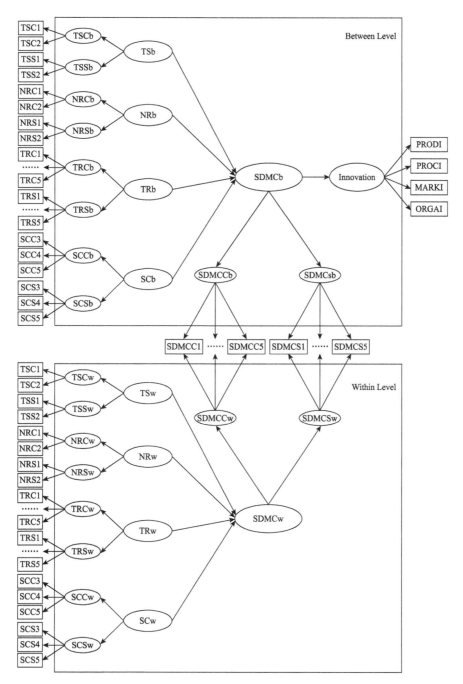

Figure 5.7 Illustration of the Model$_{multi2}$

Table 5. 25   Results of Hypotheses 1-5 of the Model$_{multi2}$

Path	Hypothesis	Level	Estimate	S. E.	p-value	Support
TS-SDMC	H1a	Within	0. 31	0. 09	0. 000	Yes
	H1b	Between	0. 29	0. 11	0. 008	Yes
NR-SDMC	H2a	Within	0. 33	0. 06	0. 000	Yes
	H2b	Between	0. 18	0. 13	0. 184	No
TR-SDMC	H3a	Within	−0. 38	0. 06	0. 000	Yes
	H3b	Between	−0. 83	0. 10	0. 000	Yes
SC-SDMC	H4a	Within	0. 10	0. 06	0. 100	No
	H4b	Between	−0. 19	0. 14	0. 157	No
SDMC-Innovation	H5	Between	−0. 84	0. 04	0. 000	Yes

Table 5. 26 presents the results of testing the mediation at the between-level, in terms of Hypotheses 6(1) -6(4). In this table, the a path reflects the relationship between social capital and social decision-making constraints, the b path reflects the relationships between social decision-making constraints and innovation, the c path reflects the direct effects of social capital on innovation, and the indirect effects ($a * b$) represent the mediation effects. Mediation is supported when the indirect effect for a given model is statistically significant, with full mediation supported when the indirect effect ($a * b$) is significant and the direct (c) path is not significant (Hodgkinson and Starbuck 2008). Accordingly, the results suggest that social decision-making constraints fully mediate the relationship between tie strength and innovation and partially mediates the relationship between trust and innovation at the between-level.

Table 5.26   Results of Hypotheses 6(1) - (4) of the Model$_{multi2}$

Hypothesis	Path a		Path b		Path c		Indirect effects		Mediated
	Estimate	p-value	Estimate	p-value	Estimate	p-value	Estimate	p-value	
H6(1) TS – SDMC – Innovation	0.29 (0.11)	0.008	-0.84 (0.04)	0.000	-0.15 (0.11)	0.161	-0.25	0.008	Fully
H6(2) NR – SDMC – Innovation	0.18 (0.13)	0.184	-0.84 (0.04)	0.000	-0.19 (0.11)	0.098	-0.15	0.191	No
H6(3) TR – SDMC – Innovation	-0.83 (0.06)	0.000	-0.84 (0.04)	0.000	0.22 (0.09)	0.009	0.69	0.000	Partially
H6(4) SC – SDMC – Innovation	-0.19 (0.14)	0.157	-0.84 (0.04)	0.000	0.09 (0.13)	0.492	0.16	0.159	No

Note: Path a = path from social capital to social decision – making constraints; path b = path from social decision – making constraints to innovation; path c = path from social capital to innovation; indirect effects = $a * b$. Mediation supported when indirect effects are significant. Full mediation supported when indirect effects are significant and path c is not significant. S. E. in parentheses.

5. 7   Moderating effects of power distance and high-low context

This section aims to present the results of the moderating effects of power distance and high-low context. The measurement model of the two moderators in terms of power distance and high-low context need to be evaluated separately. Therefore, following the two stages in terms of the measurement model and SEM, the test of the moderating effects consists of the following two stage processes: (1) evaluate the measurement model of power distance and high-low context, and (2) test the moderating effects with cross-group methods.

5. 7. 1   Measurement model evaluation of power distance and high-low context

Along with the previous process of the measurement model evaluation of $Model_{multi2}$, this stage involves three steps.

Table 5. 27   Fit indices from the CFA, $Model_{ml}$

CFA Model	χ^2	df	χ^2/df	CFI	TLI	RMSEA	SRMR
$Model_{ml}$	815. 67	53	15. 39	0. 80	0. 74	0. 09	0. 04

To begin with, the conventional CFA is attempted, suggesting some potential refinements. As shown in Table 5. 27, the conventional CFA analysis with the original full scales of moderators ($Model_{ml}$) indicates a poor model fit. When factor loadings are examined (Table 5. 28), PD8, HLC1 and HLC3 are found to have small factor loadings with the corresponding latent variables.

Table 5. 28   Standard factor loadings from CFA, $Model_{ml}$

Item	Construct	
	Power distance	High-low context
PD1	0. 61	
PD2	0. 49	
PD3	0. 55	
PD4	0. 66	
PD5	0. 65	
PD6	0. 49	
PD7	0. 70	

123

continued

Item	Construct	
	Power distance	High-low context
PD8	0. 29	
HLC1		0. 53
HLC2		0. 58
HLC3		0. 50
HLC4		0. 53

However, as discussed previously, the conventional single-level CFA fails to incorporate the hierarchical nature of the data. Therefore, the result from the conventional CFA can only provide some potential refinements, given that the result can be influenced by firm-level factor structure with substantial systemic between-group variance. Therefore, the second step is to calculate the ICC, aiming to provide the justification for the appropriateness of multilevel analysis. As shown in Table 5. 29, the ICC's range of each item is from 0. 21 to 0. 47. The relatively high values of ICC suggest its appropriateness for the measurement model with MCFA.

Table 5. 29   ICC values of each item of the moderators

Item	Construct	
	Power distance	High-low context
PD1	0. 32	
PD2	0. 25	
PD3	0. 30	
PD4	0. 34	
PD5	0. 36	
PD6	0. 21	
PD7	0. 37	
PD8	0. 28	
HLC1		0. 47
HLC2		0. 35
HLC3		0. 40
HLC4		0. 33

Having justified the appropriateness of MCFA, the final step is to perform MCFA to simultaneously estimate the within- and between-level model of moderators ($Model_{m2}$). Table 5. 30 presents the results of the MCFA, suggesting a relatively poor fit for the data.

Table 5. 30　　Fit indices from MCFA, $Model_{m2}$

MSEM	χ^2	df	χ^2/df	CFI	TLI	RMSEA	SRMR	
							Within	Between
$Model_{m2}$	437. 38	106	4. 13	0. 80	0. 75	0. 05	0. 03	0. 26

From the conventional CFA, the item of PD8 does not load well. Likewise, PD8 is found to have a small factor loading with the corresponding latent variables at both the within- and between-level from MCFA (see Table 5. 31). PD8 refers to the questions of "A company's rules should not be broken—not even when the employee thinks it is in the company's best interest". From the theoretical perspective in Section 2. 5, even individuals with the cultural value of low power distance, they are more likely to discuss the policies and rules of the firm, but not break the rules. 83. 9 percent of respondents in this study believe that the company's rules should not be broken (the little variance in the responses to the items negatively impacts on the factor loading). Therefore, PD8 has been deleted at both the within- and between-level in this study.

Table 5. 31　Standard factor loadings at the within- and between-level from MCFA, $Model_{m2}$

Item	Construct at within-level		Construct at between-level	
	Power distance	High-low context	Power distance	High-low context
PD1	0. 41		0. 90	
PD2	0. 49		0. 49	
PD3	0. 49		0. 62	
PD4	0. 51		0. 88	
PD5	0. 47		0. 93	
PD6	0. 52		0. 48	
PD7	0. 50		0. 98	
PD8	0. 39		0. 05	

continued

Item	Construct at within-level		Construct at between-level	
	Power distance	High-low context	Power distance	High-low context
HLC1		0. 27		0. 42
HLC2		0. 48		1. 00
HLC3		0. 35		0. 33
HLC4		0. 43		0. 91

Furthermore, by examining the correlation among the four items of the construct of high-low context (shown in Table 5. 32), it is found that HLC1 and HLC3 are well correlated, and HLC2 and HLC4 are also well correlated, but the correlations across the two groups are substantially low.

This study also aims to measure individuals' communication styles in the work context. Yet the items of HLC1 and HLC3 refer to the questions "Honesty is valued in meetings and discussions" and "I like to say it as it is", respectively. These two questions are more likely to focus on the personal qualities of an individual, beyond the communication style. Whereas, HLC2 and HLC4 refer to "I usually try to avoid showing disagreement openly in a discussion because we prefer to maintain a sense of harmony in meetings" and "I believe that maintaining harmony and positive tone in a meeting is more important than speaking honestly", which explicitly ask questions about the communication style in the workplace. Therefore, when factor loadings are examined at both the within- and between-level, HLC1 and HLC3 are found to have small factor loadings, and thus have been eliminated from the study.

Table 5. 32   Correlation between four items of high-low context

	HLC1	HLC2	HLC3	HLC4
HLC1	1. 00			
HLC2	0. 22	1. 00		
HLC3	0. 45	0. 23	1. 00	
HLC4	0. 21	0. 43	0. 17	1. 00

5. 7. 2   Moderating effects of power distance and high-low context

With the refined items of the construct of power distance and high-low context, this section tests moderating effects of the two constructs by adopting the cross-group method. Specifically, when examining the moderating effects of power distance and high-low context, the final data (1, 007 individual-responses with 102 firm-responses) are used for the analysis after applying the method for determining responses into three groups:

 - "high power distance"/ "high context" group (half standard deviation above the mean);

 - "low power distance"/ "low context" group (half standard deviation below the mean);

 - the middle group (between the two half standard deviation).

Only the "high power distance"/ "high context" and "low power distance"/ "low context" groups are used for analysis. The approach to dividing the continuous variables into three groups and only using the two extreme groups for analysis can result in lower statistical power with a smaller sample size. However, according to Gelman and Park (2009), compared with the traditional binary-split approach such an approach can maintain reasonably high statistical power to yield a better communication of the results and understanding of the effects.

Table 5. 33   Descriptive statistics of two groups of power distance and high-low context

	N	Mean	Std. Deviation
High power distance	388	5. 22	0. 41
Low power distance	374	3. 36	0. 38
High context	420	5. 82	0. 39
Low context	307	4. 14	0. 52

The descriptive statistics of the "high power distance" and "low power distance" groups, "high context" and "low context" groups are presented in Table 5. 33. The two groups of power distance (the mean $=5. 22$ for the high power distance group, the mean $=3. 36$ for the low power distance group) and the high-low context (the mean $=5. 82$ for high context, the mean $=4. 14$ for low context) to be contrasted are very distinct.

1. *The moderating effects of power distance*

The previous results of Model$_{multi2}$ (Table 5. 25 in Section 5. 65) shed some important light on the relationships between social capital and social decision-making constraints. This section focuses on whether further refinement is desirable through the investigation of possible moderating effects of power distance and high-low context. Firstly, Table 5. 34 presents the fit indices of two models with the data from the "high power distance" group and "low power distance" group, representing Model$_{hp}$ and Model$_{lp}$, respectively. With a smaller sample size, the fit indices of two models are not as good as that of Model$_{multi2}$, but they are all at an acceptable level.

Table 5. 34   Fit indices of Model$_{hp}$ and Model$_{lp}$

Model	χ^2	df	χ^2/df	CFI	TLI	RMSEA	SRMR	
							Within	Between
Model$_{hp}$	1074. 03	785	1. 37	0. 93	0. 93	0. 03	0. 05	0. 11
Model$_{lp}$	1063. 02	785	1. 35	0. 95	0. 94	0. 03	0. 05	0. 13

Moreover, Table 5. 35 presents the parameter estimates for the two-group comparison of high and low power distance, showing that the previous results differ somewhat across groups characterized by different extents of power distance. However, the results shown in Table 5. 31 are largely non-significant, indicating that Hypotheses 7a(1), 7a(2) and 7a(4) and Hypotheses 7b(1), 7b(2) and 7b(4) are not supported.

However, in both the "high power distance" group and "low power distance" group, the effects of trust on social decision-making constraints at both the within- and between-level are found to be significant. Hypothesis 7a(3) and Hypothesis 7b(3) assume that power distance can negatively moderate the effects of trust on social decision-making constraints at the individual- and firm-level, expecting that in the "high power distance" group, the influence of trust on social decision making-constraints is weaker; yet such influence is strengthened in the "low power distance" group at both levels. In relation to the results, it is found that at the within-level, the effect of trust on social decision-making constraints becomes stronger ($\beta = -0.51$, p <0. 050) in the "low power distance" group than in the Model$_{multi2}$ ($\beta = -0.38$, p <0. 001), providing support for Hypothesis 7a(3) in the "low power distance" group. Yet this same hypothesis is not supported in the "high power distance" group, due to the path coefficient in the "high power distance" group ($\beta = -0.38$, p <0. 050) being almost identical to the result in Model$_{multi2}$ ($\beta = -0.38$, p < 0. 001). Accordingly, Hypothesis

7a (3) is partially supported.

Likewise, at the between-level, the path coefficient between trust and social decision making constraints in the "high power distance" group ($\beta = -0.73$, p <0.001) is less than in $Model_{multi2}$ ($\beta = -0.83$, p <0.001), showing that the between-level effect of trust on social decision making-constraints becomes weaker with high-level power distance (in support of Hypothesis 7b(3)). Yet the moderating effect of trust on social decision-making constraints in low power distance at the between-level is not in the hypothesized direction. The relationship between trust and social decision-making constraints in the "low power distance" group ($\beta = -0.51$, p <0.050) is weaker than in the $Model_{multi2}$ ($\beta = -0.83$, p <0.001). Therefore, Hypothesis 7b(3) is partially supported.

Table 5.35   Results of the moderating effects of power distance from $Model_{hp}$ and $Model_{lp}$

Path	Level	Power distance					
		High power distance			Low power distance		
		Estimate	S. E.	P-value	Estimate	S. E.	P-value
TS-SDMC	Within	0.51	0.31	0.107	0.53	0.32	0.099
	Between	0.31	0.18	0.090	0.16	0.12	0.709
NR-SDMC	Within	0.14	0.30	0.650	0.13	0.41	0.750
	Between	0.28	0.25	0.252	0.23	0.48	0.629
TR-SDMC	Within	**-0.38** (-0.38)	0.16	0.015	**-0.51** (-0.38)	0.16	0.017
	Between	**-0.73** (-0.83)	0.14	0.000	**-0.54** (-0.83)	0.18	0.003
SC-SDMC	Within	-0.01	0.15	0.968	-0.06	0.21	0.782
	Between	-0.33	0.21	0.116	0.26	0.30	0.389

Note: The estimates in bold indicate the significant results in $Model_{hp}$ and $Model_{lp}$.

The estimates in brackets are from the results by testing $Model_{multi2}$ in Table 5.21.

2. The moderating effects of high-low context

Table 5.36 shows the fit indices of $Model_{hc}$ and $Model_{lc}$ with the data from the "high context" group and the "low context" group, respectively. Even though the fit indices of $Model_{hc}$ and $Model_{lc}$ are not as good as those of $Model_{multi2}$ (due to the smaller sample size), they are still acceptable.

Table 5.36　　　　　Fit indices of $Model_{hc}$ and $Model_{lc}$

MSEM	χ^2	df	χ^2/df	CFI	TLI	RMSEA	SRMR	
							Within	Between
$Model_{hc2}$	1144.26	785	1.46	0.92	0.92	0.03	0.05	0.09
$Model_{lc2}$	1133.46	785	1.44	0.90	0.90	0.03	0.05	0.09

Furthermore, the parameter estimates for the two-group comparison of high and low context communication style are presented in Table 5.37, suggesting that previous results differ somewhat across groups characterized by different extents of high-low context.

Table 5.37　　　Results of the moderating effects of high-low context

Path	Level	High-low context					
		High context			Low context		
		Estimate	S.E.	P-value	Estimate	S.E.	P-value
TS-SDMC	Within	**0.52** (0.31)	0.09	0.000	0.15	0.23	0.528
	Between	0.16	0.15	0.276	0.33	0.52	0.522
NR-SDMC	Within	**0.28** (0.33)	0.10	0.005	**0.47** (0.33)	0.22	0.003
	Between	0.19	0.21	0.359	0.12	0.51	0.807
TR-SDMC	Within	-0.25	0.13	0.058	**-0.38** (-0.38)	0.12	0.022
	Between	**-0.71** (-0.83)	0.17	0.000	**-0.68** (-0.83)	0.16	0.000
SC-SDMC	Within	-0.01	0.15	0.982	0.07	0.15	0.636
	Between	-0.02	0.22	0.919	-0.11	0.53	0.842

Note: The estimates in bold represent the significant results in $Model_{hc}$ and $Model_{lc}$.
The estimates in brackets are from the results by testing $Model_{multi2}$ in Table 5.21.

Hypothesis 8a and 8b assume that the effects of (1) tie strength, (2) norm of reciprocity, (3) trust and (4) shared cognition on social decision-making constraints are negatively moderated with the extent of high-low context communication style at both the individual- and firm-level, specifically expecting that such relationships are weaker in the "high context" group and stronger in the "low context" group at the both the within- and between-level. Results shown in Ta-

ble 5. 36 indicate that the moderating effects of high-low context on the relationship between shared cognition and social decision-making constraints are not significant in both the "high context" group and "low context" group at both the
within- and between-level, and thus Hypotheses 8a(4) and 8b(4) are not supported. Likewise, as the results are not significant, Hypotheses 8b(1) and 8b(2)
are not supported.

Furthermore, at the within-level, the path coefficient between tie strength
and social decision-making constraints in the "high context" group (β =0. 52, p
<0. 001) is larger than in the Model$_{multi2}$ (β = $-0. 31$, p <0. 001), indicating
that the effect of tie strength on social decision-making constraints becomes stronger with high context communication, which is the opposite to the hypothesized
direction. In addition, the result is not significant in the "low context" group,
indicating that Hypothesis 8a(1) is not supported.

Moreover, compared to the path coefficient between norm of reciprocity
and social decision-making constraints at the within-level in Model$_{multi2}$ (β =
$-0. 33$, p <0. 001), the path coefficient in the "high context" group (β =
0. 28, p <0. 010) is less, while the path coefficient in the "low context" group
(β =0. 47, p <0. 010) is larger. Therefore, the individual-level effect of norm
of reciprocity on social decision-making constraints becomes weaker as the extent
of context increased, thus providing support for Hypothesis 8a(2) in both "high
context" and "low context" groups.

Regarding the relationship between trust and social decision-making constraints, the path coefficients in the "low context" group are less at both the within-level (β = $-0. 38$, p <0. 050) and between-level (β = $-0. 68$, p <0. 001)
than in Model$_{multi2}$ (β = $-0. 38$, p <0. 001 at the within-level and β = $-0. 83$,
p <0. 001 at the between-level), which are the opposite to the hypothesized
direction. Therefore, H8a (3) is not supported, given that the relationship
between trust and social decision-making constraints is not significant at the
between-level in the "high context" group. However, the path coefficient in the
"high context" group at the between-level (β = $-0. 71$, p <0. 001) is less than
in Model$_{multi2}$ (β = $-0. 83$, p <0. 001), indicating that the effect of trust on social decision-making constraints become less with a high context communication
style. Thus, H8b(3) is partially supported.

Accordingly, Table 5. 38 and Table 5. 39 summarise tested moderating
effects of power distance and high-low context. Generally, most of the moderation hypotheses are not supported due to the statistical non-significant and opposite direction of the hypotheses.

Table 5.38   Tested moderation hypotheses of power distance

Path	Level	Hypothesis	Power distance High	Power distance Low	Support
TS-SDMC	Within	H7a(1)	0.51	0.53	No
	Between	H7b(1)	0.31	0.16	No
NR-SDMC	Within	H7a(2)	0.14	0.13	No
	Between	H7b(2)	0.28	0.23	No
TR-SDMC	Within	H7a(3)	−0.38 *	**−0.51** *	Partially
	Between	H7b(3)	**−0.73** ***	−0.54 **	Partially
SC-SDMC	Within	H7a(4)	−0.01	−0.06	No
	Between	H7b(4)	−0.33	0.26	No

Note: The estimates with bold fonts indicate the support to the hypotheses.
***significant at the $p < 0.001$ level
**significant at $p < 0.010$ level
* significant at $p < 0.050$ level

Hypotheses 7a(3) and 7b(3) are significant at both the "high power distance" and "low power distance" groups; however, given that the path coefficient does not change enough or the direction is opposite to the hypothesized direction, the two hypotheses are only partially supported.

Accordingly, only Hypothesis 8a(2) is supported, implying that the high-low context negatively moderates the relationship between norm of reciprocity and social decision-making constraints at the individual-level. Hypothesis 8b(3) is partially supported, due to the opposite direction from the hypothesis in the "low context" group.

Table 5.39   Tested moderation hypotheses of high-low context

Path	Level	Hypothesis	High-low context High context	High-low context Low context	Support
TS-SDMC	Within	H8a(1)	0.52 ***	0.15	No
	Between	H8b(1)	0.16	0.33	No
NR-SDMC	Within	H8a(2)	**0.28** **	**0.47** **	Yes
	Between	H8b(2)	0.19	0.12	No
TR-SDMC	Within	H8a(3)	−0.25	−0.38 *	No
	Between	H8b(3)	**−0.71** ***	−0.68 ***	Partially
SC-SDMC	Within	H8a(4)	−0.01	0.07	No
	Between	H8b(4)	−0.02	−0.11	No

Note: The estimates with bold fonts indicate the support to the hypotheses.
*** significant at the $p < 0.001$ level
** significant at $p < 0.010$ level
* significant at $p < 0.050$ level

5. 8   Summary

This chapter presents the statistical results of the hypotheses emanating from the multilevel model. Multilevel structural equation modelling (MSEM) using Mplus has been chosen to test the measurement and structural model. The MSEM analysis is performed in two stages. In the first stage, multilevel confirmatory factor analysis (MCFA) has been employed. In addition to assess the fit of the measurement model, which is the purpose of conventional CFA, this chapter formally tests the important issue pertaining to the independence of constructs due to the hierarchical structure of the data employed in this study. Assessment of results indicates the appropriateness of the multilevel analysis for the data due to the high ICC values. However, the measurement model needs to be rectified with relatively moderated fit indices from MCFA (χ^2/df = 1. 62, CFI = 0. 93, TLI = 0. 92, RMSEA = 0. 02, and $SRMR_{within}$ = 0. 03, $SRMR_{between}$ = 0. 10). Therefore, the items SCC1 SCS1 SCC2 and SCS2, which have a low degree of standard factor loadings from both conventional CFA and MCFA, are dropped. After dropping these problematic items, MCFA is performed again for the measurement model. The results of the refined model reveal that the fit indices have been improved, demonstrating an acceptable fit for the data (χ^2/df = 1. 48, CFI = 0. 95, TLI = 0. 95, RMSEA = 0. 02, and $SRMR_{within}$ = 0. 03, $SRMR_{between}$ =0. 06).

In the second stage, the MSEM has been employed to examine the differential effects of social capital on innovation via social decision-making constraints at the within- and between-level. Five hypotheses represented as causal paths are used to examine the relationships between the latent constructs at both the within- and between-level. Following the steps of Stapleton (2013), both fit indices and parameters estimated at both levels are examined to check whether the multilevel model fitted the data and to test the hypotheses. The fit indices indicate that the multilevel model provides a good fit for the data (χ^2/df = 1. 48, CFI = 0. 95, TLI = 0. 95, RMSEA = 0. 02, and $SRMR_{within}$ = 0. 03, $SRMR_{between}$ =0. 07). However, as documented in Table 5. 39, some of hypotheses are not statistically significant. The next chapter presents a detailed discussion of the empirical results within the context of the literature so that some substantive explanations can be reached.

In addition to the hypotheses in Table 5. 40, this research also tests the moderating effects of power distance and high-low context on the relationship between social capital and social decision-making constraints. However, the moderation hypotheses are largely unsupported. The supported moderation hypotheses are presented in Table 5. 41. Regarding the partially supported hypotheses, the estimates that support the hypotheses are presented with bold fonts in Table 5. 41 below.

Table 5. 40   Summary of tested hypotheses

Hypothesis	Level	Estimate	Support
Tie strength and social decision-making constraints			
H1a	Within	**0. 31 *****	**Yes**
H1b	Between	**0. 29 ****	**Yes**
Norm of reciprocity and social decision-making constraints			
H2a	Within	**0. 33 *****	**Yes**
H2b	Between	0. 17	No
Trust and social decision-making constraints			
H3a	Within	**−0. 38 *****	**Yes**
H3b	Between	**−0. 83 *****	**Yes**
Shared cognition and social decision-making constraints			
H4a	Within	0. 10	No
H4b	Between	−0. 83	No
Social decision-making constraints and innovation			
H5	Between	**−0. 84 *****	**Yes**
Social decision-making constraints mediate tie strength and innovation			
H6(1)	Between	**−0. 25 ****	**Yes**
Social decision-making constraints mediate norm of reciprocity and innovation			
H6(2)	Between	−0. 15	No
Social decision-making constraints mediate trust and innovation			
H6(3)	Between	**0. 69 *****	**Partially**
Social decision-making constraints mediate shared cognition and innovation			
H6(4)	Between	0. 16	No

*** significant at the $p < 0.001$ level
** significant at $p < 0.010$ level
* significant at $p < 0.050$ level

Table 5.41　Summary of supported moderation hypotheses

Path	Level	Hypothesis	Power distance		Support
			High	Low	
Trust and social decision-making constraints	Within	H7a(3)	−0.38 *	−0.51 *	Partially
	Between	H7b(3)	−0.73 ***	−0.54 **	Partially

Path	Level	Hypothesis	High-low context		Support
			High	Low	
Norm of reciprocity and social decision-making constraints	Within	H8a(2)	0.28 **	0.47 **	Yes
Trust and social decision-making constraints	Between	H8b(3)	−0.71 ***	−0.68 ***	Partially

*** significant at the p <0.001 level
** significant at p <0.010 level
* significant at p <0.050 level

The next chapter discusses the above results in detail for the purpose of answering the research question outlined in Chapter One. More specifically, following the discussion of the empirical results, the next chapter draws implication from this research for both theory and practice.

Discussion

6. 1   Introduction

This chapter aims to interpret the results reported in the previous chapter, and in so doing, to answer the research questions at the core of this study.

The chapter is divided into four sections. Following the introduction, Section 6. 2 provides detailed explanations of the empirical findings. Theoretical and managerial implications of the findings are illustrated in Section 6. 3. Finally, Section 6. 4 highlights the key issues pertaining to the current chapter.

6. 2   Discussion of the empirical results

Based on the summary of the tested hypotheses (Table 6. 1), the supported relationships are presented in Figure 6. 1. A side-by-side comparison of Figure 6. 1 and Figure 3. 2 (the proposed multilevel model in Section 5. 5. 3) allows for an understanding of which hypotheses are supported by the empirical data.

6. 2. 1   Social decision-making constraints as a mediator

This section explains the results of the tested hypotheses related to the relationship between social capital and social decision-making constraints at both individual and firm levels, aiming to answer the following specific research question:

> What is the mediating role of social decision-making constraints in the relationships between individual- and firm-level social capital and firm-level innovation performance?

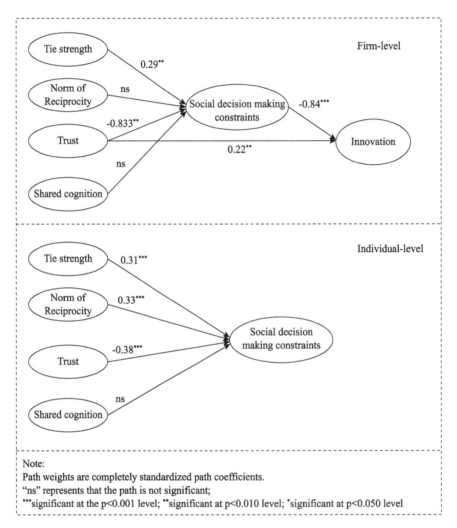

Figure 6.1   Supported relationships in the model

Table 6. 1　　　　　　　**Summary of tested hypotheses**

Hypothesis	Level	Support
Tie strength and social decision-making constraints		
H1a	Individual	Yes
H1b	Firm	Yes
Norm of reciprocity and social decision-making constraints		
H2a	Individual	Yes
H2b	Firm	No
Trust and social decision-making constraints		
H3a	Individual	Yes
H3b	Firm	Yes
Shared cognition and social decision-making constraints		
H4a	Individual	No
H4b	Firm	No
Social decision-making constraints and innovation		
H5	Firm	Yes
Social decision-making constraints mediate tie strength and innovation		
H6(1)	Firm	Yes
Social decision-making constraints mediate norm of reciprocity and innovation		
H6(2)	Firm	No
Social decision-making constraints mediate trust and innovation		
H6(3)	Firm	Partially
Social decision-making constraints mediate shared cognition and innovation		
H6(4)	Firm	No
Power distance moderates the relationship between tie strength and social decision-making constraints		
H7a(1)	Individual	No
H7b(1)	Firm	No
Power distance moderates the relationship between norm of reciprocity and social decision-making constraints		
H7a(2)	Individual	No
H7b(2)	Firm	No
Power distance moderates the relationship between trust and social decision-making constraints		
H7a(3)	Individual	Partially
H7b(3)	Firm	Partially

continued

Hypothesis	Level	Support
Power distance moderates the relationship between shared cognition and social decision-making constraints		
H7a(4)	Individual	No
H7b(4)	Firm	No
High-low context moderates the relationship between tie strength and social decision-making constraints		
H8a(1)	Individual	No
H8b(1)	Firm	No
High-low context moderates the relationship between norm of reciprocity and social decision-making constraints		
H8a(2)	Individual	Yes
H8b(2)	Firm	No
High-low context moderates the relationship between trust and social decision-making constraints		
H8a(3)	Individual	Partially
H8b(3)	Firm	Partially
Power distance moderates the relationship between shared cognition and social decision-making constraints		
H8a(4)	Individual	No
H8b(4)	Firm	No

1. Tie strength, social decision-making constraints and innovation

Previous studies tend to concern themselves with social capital as a single level of analysis, this study, however, applies a multilevel approach to fragment social capital into individual- and firm-level to examine their impacts on firms' innovation performance. The empirical results from Section 5.6 indicate that tie strength, as the sub-construct of structural social capital, can increase the social decision-making constraints at both the individual- and the firm-level, which, in turn, harm the firm's innovation performance.

In addition to the overall positive effect of tie strength, previous studies have indicated that the relationship between tie strength and innovation exhibits differentials. For example, an inverted U-shape relationship between tie strength and innovation has been discovered by Leenders et al. (2003) and McFadyen and Cannella (2004). The curvilinear relationship suggests the presence of the negative effects of tie strength on innovation, but such studies have not provided empirical evidence regarding which specific negative outcome of tie strength impedes innovation. Moreover, theoretically, Perry-Smith (2006) and Chung and Jackson (2013) claim that a high-level of tie strength can facilitate mutual interde-

139

pendence, and thus leads to little room for autonomy, yet few studies provide empirical support for this argument. The results of this study not only confirm the notion that it is not always true that tie strength can enhance innovation performance, but also answer the question regarding which specific negative outcome of tie strength harms innovation. That is, as strong ties produce demands for conformity, tie strength negatively influences innovation performance through the route of social decision-making constraints. Therefore, moderate levels of interaction frequency and closeness among individuals are necessary for optimal levels of innovation.

2. Norm of reciprocity, social decision-making constraints and innovation

Regarding the effect of norm of reciprocity on social decision-making constraints, the empirical findings indicate that, at the individual-level, the norm of reciprocity between two individuals exhibits a significant and positive impact on social decision-making constraints between two such individuals. However, at the firm-level, the empirical findings demonstrate that the mediating role of social decision-making constraints between norm of reciprocity and innovation performance is not significant, due to the insignificant relationship between norm of reciprocity and social decision-making constraints. Plausibly, although this study predicts that the norm of reciprocity can affect social decision-making constraints equally at the individual- and firm-level, the results indicate that the assumption that individual- and firm-level perceptions operate equivalently is not always accurate.

Likewise, when adopting a multilevel approach to investigate the impacts of social capital at different levels on an individual's knowledge sharing, the insignificant results regarding the team cooperative norms are also proposed for inclusion by Yu et al. (2013). In their study, the results reveal that an individual's affective commitment can enhance his/her knowledge sharing. However, at the team-level, the team cooperative norm, which is measured by aggregating individuals' ratings to the team level, is shown to have an insignificant impact on individuals' explicit knowledge. Thus, it should be noted that the predictive power of individual- and firm-level perceptions may differ depending on the construct of interest (Kiersch 2012).

3. Trust, social decision-making constraints and innovation

In this study, among all sub-constructs of the three dimensions of social capital, trust is the only one that reduces social decision-making constraints at both the individual and firm levels. The negative relationship is in accordance with the findings from Li et al's (2013) studies, demonstrating that trust can help to reduce the constraints on decision-making. In addition, this study extends Li et al's

(2013) argument by using a multilevel approach to examine such a relationship at both the individual- and firm-level, and to examine the mediating effect of social decision-making constraints on trust and innovation at the firm-level. The empirical findings in this study indicate that social decision-making constraints partially mediate the relationship between trust and innovation performance at the firm-level, considering that the direct relationship between trust and innovation performance is positive and significant.

In the context of innovation, trust plays a prominently positive role. This argument has been widely accepted in previous studies (Zheng 2010). Among the empirical studies concerning the direct relationship between trust and innovation, it has been consistently found that trust generally contributes to innovation. For example, in a study by Moran (2005), product and process innovation can be increased when sales managers enjoy a high level of trust with their contacts. Kulkarni and Ramamoorthy (2017) further confirm the positive relationship between trust and a firm's innovation performance in Chinese manufacturing firms. Regarding the indirect relationship between trust and innovation, trust is believed to positively affect innovation by promoting learning and reducing knowledge tacitness (Wicker 1979), facilitating the process of knowledge transfer (Nutt 2010), and increasing affective commitment (Kraatz 1998). In this study, trust is the only construct that has a directly positive and significant effect on innovation. The total effect of trust on innovation is 0.809, demonstrating the influential power of trust on innovation. Moreover, this study not only confirms the direct effect of trust on innovation, but also improves the existing literature by empirically highlighting the mediating role of social decision-making constraints. This empirical finding can answer the question regarding how trust fosters innovation. That is, achieving a high level trusting relationship among firm members can reduce a specific barrier to firm innovation—social decision-making constraints.

4. Shared cognition, social decision-making constraints and innovation

In this research, the proposed model hypothesizes that shared cognition has a positive effect on social decision-making constraints at both individual and firm levels. However, there is no convincing evidence to support these hypotheses from the empirical findings. With regard to the insignificant results, following plausible reasons may explain such results. Firstly, it is difficult to define and measure shared cognition, given that the terminologies used in shared cognition are scattered. In a study which reviews 10 years of research on cognition, Walsh (1995) indicates that approximately 80 terms (e.g. "managerial perception", "organizational ideologies" and "frames of reference") were used to represent cognition. Recently, more terms have been used to represent cognition, specifically including shared vision (Tsai and Ghoshal 1998), goal congruence (Jap and Anderson 2003), schemas (Elsbach et al. 2005) and cognitive framework (Phipps et al. 2013). Therefore, it is difficult to identify cognition as the centre of the research, because cognitive forms are dynamic and multi-perspective, rather than static and singular. This is the reason that, in Zheng's (2010) review of the effects of social capital on innovation, the search for literature concerning the relationship between shared cognition and innovation has been much more difficult than for the other dimensions of social capital.

Moreover, several empirical studies reveal that the effects of cognitive social capital often are insignificant. For example, Tsai and Ghoshal's (1998) study reveals that there is no significant influence of shared vision on innovation. When examining the effects of cognitive social capital on strategic and operational performance, Villena et al's study (2011) fails to provide empirical evidence to confirm the hypothesis regarding cognitive social capital. The explanation of the result is that participating firms in the study have not achieved a high level of shared vision, and thus may not have reached the threshold point. The insignificant results regarding the effect of cognitive social capital are also reported by Yu et al. (2013), who use a multilevel approach to investigate the impacts of social capital at different levels on an individual's knowledge sharing. The results reveal that, at the individual level, individuals' perceptions of shared cognition with other members can enhance their knowledge sharing in the team. However, at the team level, team cognitive capital, indicated by the commonality and sharedness of team members' cognition, is revealed to have an insignificant impact on individuals' knowledge sharing. Similarly to the construct of norm of reciprocity, the predictive power of shared cognition at individual and firm levels is likely to be different. Therefore, all the conditions mentioned above warrant further investigation in regard to cognitive social capital by calling for a renewed definition that incorporates multiplicity and dynamism, in addition to an innovative approach to measurement.

6.2.2 Culture as a moderator

This section explains the results of testing the hypotheses related to the moderating effects of power distance and high-low context on the relationship between social capital and social decision-making constraints at both individual and firm levels, for the purpose of answering the research question:

How does culture influence the relationships between social capital and social deci-

sion-making constraints at both individual- and firm- level?

As presented in Section 5. 7. 2, the results have largely failed to support the moderating effects of power distance and high-low context on the relationships between social capital and social decision-making constraints at both levels of individual and firm. Regarding the moderating effects of power distance, only two hypotheses were found to be partially significant; one was at the individual level, and the other was at the firm level. Regarding the moderating effects of high-low context, only one hypothesis was found to be statistically significant at the individual level, and one hypothesis was partially supported at the firm level.

There are two plausible interpretations of the largely non-significant moderation effects of power distance and high-low context. Firstly, one possible explanation is that the sample in each group was not sufficiently large. The entire data set to test $Model_{multi2}$ was comprised of 1, 007 employees, indicating a good fit to the data (χ^2/df =1. 48, CFI =0. 95, TLI =0. 95, RMSEA =0. 02, and $SRMR_{within}$ = 0. 03, $SRMR_{between}$ =0. 07). However, when examining the moderating effects of power distance, the sample size in the high power distance group to test $Model_{hpd}$ was 388, and the sample size for the low power distance group to test $Model_{lpd}$ was 374. Likewise, when examining the moderating effects of high-low context, the sample size for the high context group to test $Model_{hc}$ was 420, whereas the sample size for the low context group to test $Model_{lc}$ was 307. Therefore, with a smaller sample size, even though the fit indices of $Model_{hpd}$, $Model_{lpd}$, $Model_{hc}$, and $Model_{lc}$ were at an acceptable level, they were not as good as those of $Model_{multi2}$. This may provide a challenge in terms of achieving the expected results by testing the model.

Secondly, according to Tangpong et al. (2016), demographic characteristics may help to explain why scholars can find significant effects for culture values for a specific outcome in one study yet fail to find such effects in another. According to a meta-analysis involving 598 empirical articles, theses, conference presentations and unpublished studies, Taras et al. (2016) specify the conditions under which cultural values tend to have more meaningful influences on relevant organizational outcomes. They indicate that the predictive power of cultural values, such as power distance, is significantly stronger for older, rather than younger respondents. This argument is rooted in the concept of traitedness (Abbink et al. 2002). Traited individuals can identify themselves with a given trait, and can process a strong internal representation of a trait. They are likely to act in a consistent way across different situations (Shang et al. 2008; Swärd 2016). Expressed simply, "they know who they are" (Tangpong et al. 2016, p. 408). In addition, the cultural values of younger individuals are more malleable than those of older individuals, but, as individuals age, traitedness with respect to cultural values increases (Uhl-Bien and Maslyn 2003). Therefore, older individuals, rather than younger, are likely to express more consistent attitudes and behaviours.

For this study, as revealed in Table 5.2 in Section 5.3.1 the respondents were likely to be younger individuals, rather than older. However, the effects of cultural value have been found to be significantly stronger for older, rather than younger, respondents (Tangpong et al. 2016).

In order to confirm this argument, this study used analysis of variance (ANOVA) to test the difference in means of standard deviation of the construct in terms of power distance and high-low context across ages. The standard deviation is a measure that is used to quantify the amount of variation or dispersion of a set of data values (Powell and Smith-Doerr 1994). A high standard deviation indicates that the data points are spread out over a wider range of values, while a standard deviation close to 0 indicates that the data tend to be very close to the mean. With respect to the construct of power distance, the results from the ANOVA indicate that there are significant differences in means for standard deviations of power distance across ages[1]. As indicated in Table 6.2, the general trend is that the mean of standard deviation for younger individuals is larger than for old individuals, somewhat confirming the above argument that younger individuals are less likely to have consistent attitudes and behaviours.

Table 6.2 The means for standard deviations of power distance across age

Age	Mean	N	Std. Deviation
23 −28	1.273	215	0.392
29 −35	1.173	409	0.366
29 −35	1.098	278	0.374
36 −42	1.017	91	0.430
43 −50	1.163	14	0.544

Therefore, the fact that the majority of respondents in this sample are youn-

---

[1] The mean difference is significant when the p-value is smaller than 0.05. The results from the ANOVA regarding the difference in means for standard deviations of power distance across age is $F(4, 1002)$ =3.061, p =0.016 <0.05, and the difference in means for standard deviations of high-low-context across age is $F(5.1001)$ =1.623, P =0.151 >0.05.

ger individuals may help explain the lack of significant findings regarding the moderating effects of culture in this study.

6. 3   Implications for researchers and practitioners

The implications of the findings of this study are presented under two headings: theoretical implications for researchers and managerial implications for practitioners, which are described in following sub-sections.

6. 3. 1   Theoretical implications

The results of this study have a number of significant theoretical implications. Firstly, firms have a multilevel nature due to the fact that individual members are nested in firms. The single level research that ignores the nested structure can lead to erroneous conclusions (Yu et al. 2013). This is one of the first studies to have advanced the understanding of the multilevel phenomena of social capital on innovation by properly conceptualizing and modelling firm-level social capital (including its sub-constructs and negative outcome) as the contextual effects, which are based on the aggregation of corresponding individual characteristic. With the anticipation that social capital and culture could operate at the individual- and the firm-level, the multilevel model developed for this research not only examines the effects of social capital at the individual-level, but also validates the firm-level effects of social capital on innovation with the mediating role of social decision-making constraints.

Secondly, the results yield useful insights for studies of innovation processes. Previous studies confirm that innovation process components, such as cross-functional integration, are important determinants of innovation performance (Jones and Newburn 2002; Li et al. 2017). Studies have investigated the impacts of social capital on cross-functional communication (Gu et al. 2008) and cross-functional contacts (Seibert et al. 2001). Notably, Central Document Press (1993) examine the moderating effects of social capital and decision autonomy on cross-functional collaboration and innovativeness. The results reported here are useful for innovation process research because they highlight the importance of culture, as well as the need to consider the possibility of adverse effects on innovation, such as when increased social capital becomes problematic by constraining decision-making.

Thirdly, this study contributes to social capital theory by identifying social decision-making constraints as a specific negative outcome, and analysing its mediating effects on the relationship between social capital and innovation. Scholars in the area of social capital have made repeated calls for the study regarding the negative effects of social capital in organizations (Krackhardt and Hanson 1993; Tsai and Ghoshal 1998; Inkpen and Tsang 2005; Nutt and Wilson 2010), but very few empirical efforts have responded to this call. The development and empirical analysis of the multilevel model deepens an understanding of the potentially deleterious consequence of social capital for a firm's innovation, and, in so doing, responds to recent calls for such research.

The fourth theoretical implication is that different facets of social capital might have a different effect on social decision-making constraints as a mediator to extend their respective effects on the firm's innovation. This is a new angle in social capital research. Specifically, this study offers insights into the importance of trust for promoting innovation. Moreover, although previous studies have already underlined that tie strength may exert a negative influence on innovation, and some studies have empirically indicated the quadratic relationship between tie strength and innovation, this is the first study, to the researcher's knowledge, to empirically examine and confirm one specific negative outcome of tie strength that can impede a firm's innovation performance.

Fifthly, contrary to expectations, the results have not provided support for the hypothesis that shared cognition increases social decision-making constraints at both individual- and firm-level. As Holt (2012) state, the conceptualization of a construct may diverge from culture to culture. The results reported here suggest that the Western conceptualization and measure of cognitive social capital is not operational in China. Therefore, it is suggested that a culturally-anchored conceptualization of cognitive social capital be developed. In so doing, qualitative methods are likely to prove useful.

Sixthly, this study takes culture into account by examining the moderating effects of culture on the effects of social capital with regard to social decision-making constraints. Although the results of the moderating effects are generally not statistically significant, the majority of tests are in the hypothesized direction, indicating that there is a trend towards the concept that culture strengthens or weakens the effects of social capital and social decision-making constraints. Thus, the results reported here align with the extant innovation management literature, which demonstrates that culture plays a significant moderating role in innovation (Evanschitzky et al. 2012).

Seventhly, the sample size has always been a major restriction on empirical studies. Gaining access to a large number of target respondents is a significant challenge for most researchers. This study extends the sample using the snowball sampling method after gaining the initial support from top managers of three high-technology firms in TEDA. This method has the advantage of obtaining a larger sample size within the same context.

Finally, the multilevel model was tested using MSEM. With this, both individual- and firm-level effects can be examined in parallel, with the firm-level effects being based on latent firm-level constructs formed by the aggregation of individual-level perceptions within each firm (Preacher et al. 2010). This method of inferring the firm level from individual-level indicators accounts for the error involved in cross-level inference, resulting in a more accurate representation of firm-level constructs than alternative methods of aggregate individual-level responses to the firm level. By testing the proposed multilevel model with MSEM, this study serves to promote best practice in capturing multilevel phenomena in organizational science, as well as to answer numerous calls for multilevel research in the field of innovation and social capital research (e. g. Moliterno and Mahony 2011; Payne et al. 2011; Eveleens 2017).

6. 3. 2   Managerial implications

The findings should be of particular interest to the employees and managers who work in Chinese high-tech firms. Firstly, trust has the most powerful effect on innovation. Individuals can gain a high level of freedom when making decisions if there is a trusting relationship with others. In addition, the results highlight that a trusting environment is a necessary condition for reducing the constraints on decision-making, which, in turn, facilitates innovation performance. High-technology firms generally involve a complementary mix of high technically- and commercially-skilled individuals. In order to transform creative ideas into innovation and ultimately into business success, building a trusting environment among technical and commercial individuals is the best way to effectively support their innovation ideas. The foundation of building a trusting environment is that the head of every department should seek to avoid suspicions and affective conflict with each other and with their employees in the first place. This is due to the fact that superiors are important initiators of trust, and their behaviours have a direct impact on employees' trust in their colleagues and superiors (Ng and Chua 2006).

Secondly, given the high priority afforded to social ties when conducting business in Chinese organizations (Xiao and Tsui 2007), firm members must be fully aware of the liability of strong ties. On the one hand, strong ties provide useful knowledge and scarce resources. However, the results from this study highlight the problems of developing strong ties blindly, due to the restrictions they may impose on decision-making, which can impede the acceptance and implementation of creative ideas. Especially for high-tech firms that need constant innovation, managers should work towards creating a routine and advocate an appropriate networking strategy for firm members, to enable them to ensure an appropriate level of communication frequency and closeness.

Thirdly, among the respondents, approximately one third of the individuals were associated with high power distance and high context, while another third were linked with low power distance and low context. Therefore, the managers need to be aware of their firm members' different cultural values, due to the fact that, even with a high-level trusting relationship, the social decision-making constraints may not be decreased due to high-level power distance and high-context communication. In addition, managers, particularly in a firm with high power distance cultural value, should be aware of the cultural boundaries in regard to the effective application of the theories in Western country (i. e. social capital theory), where there is likely to be a much larger concentration of individuals with a low power distance and a low-context communication style.

6. 4   Summary

The core aim of this chapter was to interpret the results reported in Chapter 5. Specifically, this chapter has provided insight into why the hypotheses are supported, and more importantly, has offered a careful interpretation regarding the findings that have deviated from the original hypotheses. Following the discussion of the results, this chapter also offered some theoretical and managerial implications. A further summary of the entire study, highlighting the contributions of this research, is outlined in Chapter 7. The relevant limitations of the research and suggestions for future study in this area are also clarified in the chapter that follows.

Conclusion

7. 1 Introduction

This chapter concludes the study by summarizing the research, including the study's findings (Section 7. 2). It also outlines the main contributions of the research from theoretical, empirical and managerial perspectives (Section 7. 3). The major limitations of the study are highlighted in Section 7. 4, whilst some suggestions for future research are provided in Section 7. 5. Finally, Section 7. 6 concludes.

7. 2 Summary of the study

Although a considerable body of research has been undertaken in the area of the social capital-innovation relationship, relatively few studies have concentrated on the negative effects of social capital on innovation. In order to develop a more objective understanding and evaluation of investment in social capital, it is necessary to consider the potential negative consequences of social capital, given that blindly promoting it can impede rather than enhance innovation performance. Moreover, firm-level innovation is at least a two-level phenomenon that involves an individual and a firm in which the individual is embedded. Yet prior studies have granted insufficient attention to the multilevel phenomenon regarding the effects of social capital on innovation. Furthermore, few studies of social capital have considered culture. Given that culture can underline individuals' behaviour, which can moderate the effects of social capital, it is imperative not to neglect the influence of culture in social capital studies. The current study addressed these issues and attempted to clarify the negative effects of social capital on innovation through the mediating role of social decision-making constraints. The study also considered how individual social capital could be aggregated into firm-level social capital.

An intensive review of prior literature was carried out in the area of innovation, social capital, social decision-making constraints and culture (Chapter 2). Following on from a review of the substantial literature, which identified a lacuna in the literature relating to the link between innovation social capital, social decision-making constraints and culture, the following research questions were addressed:

What is the mediating role of social decision-making constraints in the relationships between individual- and firm-level social capital and firm-level innovation performance?

How does culture influence the relationships between social capital and social decision-making constraints at both individual- and firm- level?

Based on the empirical and theoretical evidence gleaned from the literature, a conceptual model was developed, as detailed in Chapter 3. The model proposed the multilevel influences of social capital on innovation through social decision-making constraints, as well as the moderating effects of culture. The model depicted a total of 25 hypotheses concerning (1) how social capital influences social decision-making constraints at both individual- and firm-level; (2) how social decision-making constraints mediate the relationships between social capital and innovation performance at the firm-level; and (3) how culture moderates the relationships between social capital and social decision-making constraints at both individual- and firm-level.

Through a systematic process of construct operationalization, survey development and execution, empirical data was collected from high-technology firms in China's TEDA (Chapter 4). The empirical data was used to test the hypotheses by employing MSEM (Chapter 5). Using MSEM, both individual- and firm-level effects of social capital on social decision-making constraints were examined in parallel, with the firm-level effects based on latent firm-level variables formed by the shared variance among individual-level perceptions within each firm.

Regarding the research findings, seven hypotheses were supported, and four hypotheses were partially supported, whilst 14 hypotheses were not supported. As discussed previously (Chapter 6), this research is among the few initial attempts to examine the multilevel effects of social capital on innovation through social decision-making constraints. The findings suggest that social decision-making constraints can impede a firm's innovation performance. While tie strength increased social decision-making constraints at both individual- and firm-level, the norm of reciprocity increased social decision-making constraints at the individual-level. In contrast, trust can reduce social decision-making constraints at both levels of the individual and the firm. Moreover, the empirical study acknowledged that the relationship between shared cognition and social decision-making constraints was not statistically significant. Furthermore, it was quite interesting to note that the results largely failed to support the moderating effects of power distance and high-low context. As indicated in Section 6.2.3, the main plausible explanation was that the sample was not large enough. Overall, this study confirmed the notion that it is not always the case that social capital can enhance a firm's innovation. Rather, different facets of social capital, tie strength, norm of reciprocity and trust play varying roles in terms of affecting a firm's innovation.

7.3   Contributions of the research

This study contributes to the social capital-innovation relationship from both academic and managerial perspectives. This section discusses each of these contributions in turn.

Firstly, from the theoretical perspective, this research specifically contributes to the social capital theory by emphasizing the negative effects of social capital, in terms of social decision-making constraints. The findings of the research offer a comprehensive understanding of the impacts of social capital on innovation. In contrast to the dominant view in the literature, social capital can potentially harm innovation performance through social decision-making constraints.

Secondly, as firms are multilevel in nature – individual members nested in firms – single-level research that ignores a multilevel nested structure can lead to erroneous conclusions (Yu et al. 2013). Moreover, the development of firm-level social capital and the role of individual social capital in the development of firm-level social capital are relatively under-researched areas of study. The conceptualisation of social capital and social decision-making constraints at multilevel, with empirical support for the effects of social capital on innovation through social decision-making constraints by developing a multilevel conceptual model, constitutes an important theoretical contribution to theories of social capital and innovation. Moreover, by testing the proposed multilevel model in an MSEM framework, this study serves to promote best practice in capturing multilevel phenomena in organizational science, as well as answering numerous calls for multilevel research in social capital and innovation literature (e. g. Hitt et al. 2007; Payne et al. 2011; Eveleens 2017).

Thirdly, this study is one of the first studies that has taken account of culture in the study of social capital, and is also relatively novel in its attempt to explore the influence of culture on the effects of social capital. Thus, the third contribution made by this study is that the cultural factors, in terms of power distance and high-low context, have been added to and tested in the conceptual model.

Fourthly, given that the theoretical model was based on literature developed mainly in Western contexts, testing the theoretical model in the context of China can provide a good opportunity to evaluate the applicability of social capital theory in a different context.

The final major contribution of this research is from the managerial perspective. The research findings provide a clear understanding of costs and potential risks for individuals and firms who invest in social capital in China. Moreover, due to the importance of Chinese firms in global business, this research also provides some valuable insights for Western firms wishing to better understand Chinese firms.

As with all studies, there are also a number of limitations to the current study that require attention, as outlined in the next section.

7.4　Limitations

The findings reaped from this study need to be considered within the context of the limitations of the study, as outlined. These limitations are discussed below in terms of the context, data collection and the analytical method used to perform the analysis.

The first limitation is that employees rated the survey items of social capital, social decision-making constraints, power distance and high-low context, raising concerns regarding the potential impact of common-source variance. Nonetheless, this study also treated these above constructs as a firm-level variable, which helped to reduce possible common-source variance by aggregating responses within each firm. Moreover, common-source variance was unlikely to account for the relationships involving a firm's innovation performance that were detailed using a different source (the top managers).

Secondly, according to Muthén and Muthén (2012), it is more appropriate to use the latent variable interactions method to test moderating effects. However, due to the multilevel model of this study being rather complex, the matrices could not be inverted with the data, and thus the analysis could not be completed. Therefore, this study adopted a cross-group method to test the moderating effects. Moreover, the results may in all probability be enhanced by increasing the sample size. Additionally, given that the responses were categorized into three groups and only two of them were used for analysis, the limited sample size and the relatively large number of variables are likely to have restricted the results when testing the complex multilevel model.

7.5   Suggestions for future research

Considering the findings of this study and its contribution to knowledge, and bearing in mind the limitations listed above, this section offers a number of opportunities for future research.

Firstly, while China's TEDA was the setting for this research, the framework could potentially be applied in other Chinese cities or development areas using a similar conceptual model and survey items. To date, there are 128 National Economic and Technological Development Areas in China (Morgeson et al. 2015), and 37,211 recognized Chinese indigenous high-technology firms (Arregle et al. 2012). Although some hypotheses were found to be non-significant in the current research, one single research project does not provide sufficient evidence that this result will be broadly supported throughout China and other Eastern countries. To ensure that the theoretical model is robust and generalisable, further studies are encouraged.

Secondly, as suggested earlier in Section 6.3.1, the results are useful for innovation process research because they support the role of culture, and highlight the need to account for possible adverse effects of increased social capital. It is particularly recommended that future studies of cross-functional integration, an influential process variable, consider the boundary conditions associated with increasing social capital due to the negative effects of social decision making constraints.

Thirdly, this study considers power distance and high-low context as two moderators, and measured these two constructs at the individual level within one country. Extending the study to cover two culturally distinct countries in the analysis would allow for comparative studies. Further studies could measure power distance and high-low context at the individual-level, but should include more countries in order to ascertain the generalizability of cultural value and social capital effects beyond China.

Thirdly, in this study, as well as in previous research (e.g. Farh et al. 2007; Kirkman et al. 2009; Warner-Søderholm 2013), the reliability of power distance and high-low context were found to be marginal. Further research should pay considerable attention to the scale development of power distance and high-low context and explore more elaborate measures of these two constructs.

7.6 Conclusion

In concluding this research, this chapter presented a summary of the theoretical and empirical research undertaken in this book. In addition, it highlighted the contributions to knowledge and reviewed the limitations, as well as outlining suggestions for future research.

From the extensive review of the innovation- and social capital-related literature, this research identified a dearth of evidence regarding a multilevel approach to examine the negative influence of social capital on innovation. This gap led to the identification of social decision-making constraints as a specific negative consequence of social capital, which impedes innovation performance. Based on the literature relating to innovation, social capital, social decision-making constraints and culture, this study developed a multilevel model, which framed the analysis of the effects of social capital on innovation with the mediating role of social decision-making constraints and the moderating effects of culture. Employing a survey to collect multilevel data, this study used MSEM to analyse the data, involving 1,007 employees working at 102 high-tech firms in China's TEDA. The analysis confirmed the negative mediating role of social decision-making constraints, revealing that social capital can facilitate social decision-making at both the individual- and firm-level, which, in turn, impedes firm-level innovation.

The multilevel analysis of the social capital-innovation relationship is, therefore, a first step in an interesting research area worthy of future study. Moreover, this study not only makes important theoretical contributions; the results also have possible managerial implications. From a theoretical perspective, this study offers a comprehensive understanding of the multilevel impacts of social capital on firm innovation by providing evidence that social capital can potentially impede a firm's innovation performance. The results also suggest that individuals and firms investing in social capital need to weigh the benefits of social capital carefully against its potential costs.

References

[1] Abbink, K., Irlenbusch, B. and Renner, E. (2002) 'An Experimental Bribery Game', Journal of Law, Economics, & Organization, 18(2), 428 – 454.

[2] Adamczyk, S., Bullinger, A. C. and Möslein, K. M. (2012) 'Innovation contests: A review, classification and outlook', Creativity and Innovation Management, 21(4), 335 –360.

[3] Adhikari, K. P. and Goldey, P. (2010) 'Social capital and its "downside": the impact on sustainability of induced community-based organizations in Nepal', World Development, 38(2), 184 –194.

[4] Adler, P. S. and Kwon, S. W. (2002) 'Social capital: Prospects for a new concept', Academy of Management Review, 27(1), 17 –40.

[5] Afuah, A. (1998) Innovation Management: Strategies, Implementation, and Profits, Oxford: University Press.

[6] Alattar, L., Yates, J. F., Eby, D. W., Leblanc, D. J. and Molnar, L. J. (2016) 'Understanding and Reducing Inconsistency in Seatbelt-Use Decisions: Findings from a Cardinal Decision Issue Perspective', Risk Analysis, 36(1), 83 –97.

[7] Alexander, L. and Van Knippenberg, D. (2014) 'Teams in Pursuit of Radical Innovation: A Goal Orientation Perspective', Academy of Management Review, 39(4), 423 –438.

[8] Amabile, T. M. (1996) 'Creativity and Innovation in Organizations' in Staw, B. M. and Cummings, L. L., eds., Research in Organizational Behavior, Greenwich: CT: JAI Press, 123 –167.

[9] Amaratunga, D., Baldry, D., Sarshar, M. and Newton, R. (2002) 'Quantitative and qualitative research in the built environment: application of "mixed" research approach', Work study, 51(1), 17 –31.

[10] Amason, A. C. (1996) 'Distinguishing the effects of functional and dysfunctional conflict on strategic decision making: resolving a paradox for top management teams', Academy of Management Journal, 39(1), 123 –148.

[11] Amason, A. C. and Sapienza, H. J. (1997) 'The effects of top management team size and interaction norms on cognitive and affective conflict', Journal of Management, 23(4), 495 −516.

[12] Anderson, A. , Park, J. and Jack, S. (2007) 'Entrepreneurial Social Capital Conceptualizing Social Capital in New High-tech Firms', International Small Business Journal, 25(3), 245 −272.

[13] Anderson, J. C. and Gerbing, D. W. (1988) 'Structural equation modeling in practice: A review and recommended two-step approach', Psychological Bulletin, 103(3), 411.

[14] Arregle, J. L. , Naldi, L. , Nordqvist, M. and Hitt, M. A. (2012) 'Internationalization of Family-Controlled Firms: A Study of the Effects of External Involvement in Governance', Entrepreneurship Theory & Practice, 36 (6), 1115 −1143.

[15] Aslam, H. , Shahzad, K. , Syed, A. R. and Ramish, A. (2013) 'Social capital and knowledge sharing as determinants of academic performance', Journal of Behavioral & Applied Management, 15(1).

[16] Aslam, M. , Shahzad, K. , Syed, A. and Ramish, A. (2013) 'Social capital and knowledge sharing as determinants of academic performance', Journal of Behavior & Applied Management, 14(1), 25 −41.

[17] Atwater, L. , Wang, M. , Smither, J. W. and Fleenor, J. W. (2009) 'Are Cultural Characteristics Associated With the Relationship Between Self and Others' Ratings of Leadership?', Journal of Applied Psychology, 94 (4), 876 −886.

[18] Balogun, J. , Pye, A. and Hodgkinson, G. P. (2008) Cognitively skilled Organizational Decision Making: Making Sense of Deciding.

[19] Barbour, J. B. and Lammers, J. C. (2015) 'Measuring professional identity: a review of the literature and a multilevel confirmatory factor analysis of professional identity constructs', Journal of Professions and Organization, 2 (1), 38 −60.

[20] Baron, R. A. and Markman, G. D. (2003) 'Beyond social capital: the role of entrepreneurs' social competence in their financial success', Journal of Business Venturing, 18(1), 41 −60.

[21] Batjargal, B. (2003a) 'Social Capital and Entrepreneurial Performance in Russia: A Longitudinal Study', Organization Studies, 24(4), 535 −556.

[22] Batjargal, B. (2003b) 'Social Capital and Entrepreneurial Performance in Russia: A Longitudinal Study', Acoustics Speech & Signal Processing Newsletter IEEE, 24(4), 535 −556.

[23] Bennedsen, M. , Nielsen, K. M. , Perezgonzalez, F. and Wolfenzon, D.

(2007) 'Inside the Family Firm: The Role of Families in Succession Decisions and Performance', Quarterly Journal of Economics, 122(2), 647 – 691.

[24] Bentler, P. M. (1989) 'EQS 6 structural equations program manual', Los Angeles: BMDP Statistic Software, 86 – 102.

[25] Berrone, P. , Cruz, C. and Gomez-Mejia, L. R. (2016) 'Socioemotional Wealth in Family Firms', Family Business Review, 25(3), 258 – 279.

[26] Berthon, P. , Pitt, L. F. , Ewing, M. T. and Bakkeland, G. (2003) 'Norms and power in marketing relationships: Alternative theories and empirical evidence', Journal of Business Research, 56(9), 699 – 709.

[27] Bizzi, L. (2013) 'The Dark Side of Structural Holes A Multilevel Investigation', Journal of Management, 39(6), 1554 – 1578.

[28] Bo, B. N. and Nielsen, S. (2009) 'Learning and Innovation in International Strategic Alliances: An Empirical Test of the Role of Trust and Tacitness', Journal of Management Studies, 46(6), 1031 – 1056.

[29] Borgatti, S. P. and Cross, R. (2003) 'A relational view of information seeking and learning in social networks', Management Science, 49(4), 432 – 445.

[30] Bourdieu, P. (1986) 'The forms of capital' in Richardson, J. G. , ed. , Handbook of theory and research for the sociology of education, New York: Greenwood, 241 – 258.

[31] Bradley, S. W. , McMullen, J. S. , Artz, K. and Simiyu, E. M. (2012) 'Capital is not enough: Innovation in developing economies', Journal of Management Studies, 49(4), 694 – 717.

[32] Brass, D. J. (1995) 'A social network perspective on human resources management', Research in Personnel and Human Resources Management, 13, 39 – 79.

[33] Brass, D. J. , Galaskiewicz, J. , Greve, H. R. and Tsai, W. (2004) 'Taking Stock of Networks and Organizations: A Multilevel Perspective', Academy of Management Journal, 47(6), 795 – 817.

[34] Brislin, R. W. (1970) 'Back-translation for cross-cultural research', Journal of Cross-Cultural Psychology, 1(3), 185 – 216.

[35] Brown, T. A. (2015) Confirmatory factor analysis for applied research, Guilford Publications.

[36] Bryk, A. S. and Raudenbush, S. W. (1992) Hierarchical linear models: applications and data analysis methods, Sage Publications, Inc.

[37] Burt, R. (1992) Structural Holes: The Social Structure of Competition, Cambridge, MA: Harvard University Press.

[38] Burt, R. S. , Hogarth, R. M. and Michaud, C. (2000) 'The social capital of French and American managers', Organization Science, 11(2), 123 −147.

[39] Cao, Z. and Lumineau, F. (2015) 'Revisiting the Interplay between Contractual and Relational Governance: A Qualitative and Meta-Analytic Investigation', Journal of Operations Management, 33(1), 15 −42.

[40] Carnabuci, G. and Diószegi, B. (2015) 'Social networks, cognitive style and innovative performance: A contingency perspective', Academy of Management Journal, amj. 2013. 1042.

[41] Cavana, R. , Delahaye, B. L. and Sekeran, U. (2001) Applied business research: Qualitative and quantitative methods, John Wiley & Sons Australia.

[42] Central Document Press (1993) Selected Important Documents Since the Founding of People's Republic of China Beijing.

[43] Central Statistics Office (2012) Community Innovation Survey 2008 − 2010, Dublin, Ireland: Central Statistics Office.

[44] Chan, D. (1998) 'Functional relations among constructs in the same content domain at different levels of analysis: A typology of composition models', Journal of Applied Psychology, 83(2), 234.

[45] Chao, G. T. and Moon, H. (2005) 'The cultural mosaic: A metatheory for understanding the complexity of culture', Journal of Applied Psychology, 90(6), 1128 −1140.

[46] Chen, C. -J. and Huang, J. -W. (2007) 'How organizational climate and structure affect knowledge management—The social interaction perspective', International Journal of Information Management, 27(2), 104 −118.

[47] Chiu, C. M. , Hsu, M. H. and Wang, E. T. G. (2006) 'Understanding knowledge sharing in virtual communities: An integration of social capital and social cognitive theories', Decision Support Systems, 42(3), 1872 − 1888.

[48] Chiu, C. M. , Wang, E. T. G. , Shih, F. J. and Fan, Y. W. (2011) 'Understanding knowledge sharing in virtual communities An integration of expectancy disconfirmation and justice theories', Online Information Review, 35(1), 134 −153.

[49] Cho, J. and Dansereau, F. (2010) 'Are transformational leaders fair? A multi-level study of transformational leadership, justice perceptions, and organizational citizenship behaviors', The leadership quarterly, 21(3), 409 − 421.

[50] Chung, Y. and Jackson, S. E. (2013) 'The Internal and External Net-

works of Knowledge-Intensive Teams The Role of Task Routineness ',
Journal of Management, 39(2), 442 −468.

[51] Clercq, D. D. , Thongpapanl, N. and Dimov, D. (2009) 'When good
conflict gets better and bad conflict becomes worse: the role of social capital
in the conflict – innovation relationship', Journal of the Academy of Marketing Science, 37(3), 283 −297.

[52] Clugston, M. , Howell, J. P. and Dorfman, P. W. (2000) 'Does cultural
socialization predict multiple bases and foci of commitment? ', Journal of
Management, 26(1), 5 −30.

[53] Cohen, J. , Cohen, P. , West, S. G. and Aiken, L. S. (2013) Applied
multiple regression/correlation analysis for the behavioral sciences, Rout-
ledge.

[54] Coleman, J. (1990) Foundations of social theory, Cambridge, MA: Harvard University Press.

[55] Coleman, J. S. (1988) 'Social Capital in the Creation of Human-Capital',
American Journal of Sociology, 94, S95 − S120, available: http://
dx. doi. org/https://dx. doi. org/10. 1086/228943.

[56] Coleman, J. S. (1988) 'Social Capital in the Creation of Human Capital',
American Journal of Sociology, 94(1), 95 −120.

[57] Constant, D. , Sproull, L. and Kiesler, S. (1996) 'The kindness of stran-
gers: The usefulness of electronic weak ties for technical advice', Organization Science, 7 (2), 119 − 135, available: http://dx. doi. org/Doi
10. 1287/Orsc. 7. 2. 119.

[58] Cropanzano, R. and Mitchell, M. S. (2005) 'Social Exchange Theory:
An Interdisciplinary Review', Journal of Management, 31(6), 874 −900.

[59] Crossan, M. M. and Apaydin, M. (2010) 'A multi-dimensional framework of organizational innovation: A systematic review of the literature ',
Journal of Management Studies, 47(6), 1154 −1191.

[60] Cuevas-Rodriguez, G. , Cabello-Medina, C. and Carmona-Lavado, A.
(2014) 'Internal and External Social Capital for Radical Product Innovation: Do They Always Work Well Together? ', British Journal of Management, 25(2), 266 −284.

[61] Curran, P. J. , West, S. G. and Finch, J. F. (1996) 'The robustness of
test statistics to nonnormality and specification error in confirmatory factor
analysis', Psychological methods, 1(1), 16.

[62] Dakhli, M. and Clercq, D. D. (2004) 'Human capital, social capital, and
innovation: a multi-country study', Entrepreneurship & Regional Development, 16(2), 107 −128.

[63] Damanpour, F. and Wischnevsky, D. J. (2006) 'Research on innovation in organizations: Distinguishing innovation-generating from innovation-adopting organizations', Journal of Engineering and Technology Management, 23(4), 269 −291.

[64] Danchev, A. (2006) 'Social capital and sustainable behavior of the firm', Industrial Management & Data Systems, 106(7), 953 −965.

[65] Davis, P. S. and Harveston, P. D. (2000) 'Internationalization and Organizational Growth: The Impact of Internet Usage and Technology Involvement Among Entrepreneurled Family Businesses', Family Business Review, 13(2), 107 −120.

[66] De Clercq, D., Thongpapanl, N. and Dimov, D. (2009) 'When good conflict gets better and bad conflict becomes worse: the role of social capital in the conflict – innovation relationship', Journal of the Academy of Marketing Science, 37(3), 283 −297.

[67] Dewar, R. D. and Dutton, J. E. (1986) 'The Adoption of Radical and Incremental Innovations: An Empirical Analysis', Management Science, 32 (11), 1422 −1433.

[68] Dyer, N. G., Hanges, P. J. and Hall, R. J. (2005) 'Applying multilevel confirmatory factor analysis techniques to the study of leadership', The leadership quarterly, 16(1), 149 −167.

[69] Edmondson, A. C. and McManus, S. E. (2007) 'Methodological fit in management field research', Academy of management review, 32(4), 1246 −1264.

[70] Elliot, E. A. and Nakata, C. (2013) 'Cross-Cultural Creativity: Conceptualization and Propositions for Global New Product Development', Journal of Product Innovation Management, 30(S1), 110 −125.

[71] Elsbach, K. D., Barr, P. S. and Hargadon, A. B. (2005) 'Identifying situated cognition in organizations', Organization Science, 16(4), 422 −433.

[72] Eranova, M. and Prashantham, S. (2016) 'Decision making and paradox: Why study China?', European Management Journal, 34(3), 193 −201.

[73] Evanschitzky, H.; Eisend, M.; Calantone, R. J. and Jiang, Y. (2012) 'Success factors of product innovation: An updated meta-analysis', Journal of Product Innovation Management, 29(S1), 21 −37.

[74] Eveleens, C. (2017) Innovation management; a literature review of innovation process models and their implications.

[75] Fang, T. (2010) 'Asian management research needs more self-confidence: Reflection on Hofstede (2007) and beyond', Asia Pacific Journal of Man-

agement, 27(1), 155 −170.

[76] Farh, J. L. , Hackett, R. D. and Liang, J. (2007) 'Individual-level cultural values as moderators of perceived organizational support-employee outcome relationships in China: Comparing the effects of power distance and traditionality', Academy of Management Journal, 50(3), 715 −729.

[77] Filieri, R. , McNally, R. C. , O'Dwyer, M. and O'Malley, L. (2014) 'Structural social capital evolution and knowledge transfer: Evidence from an Irish pharmaceutical network', Industrial Marketing Management, 43(3), 429 −440.

[78] Fulmer, C. A. and Gelfand, M. J. (2012) 'At What Level (and in Whom) We Trust', Journal of Management, 38(4), 1167 −1230.

[79] Gómez-Mejía, L. R. , Cruz, C. , Berrone, P. and Castro, J. D. (2011) 'The Bind That Ties: Socioemotional Wealth Preservation in Family Firms', Academy of Management Annals, 5(1), 653 −707.

[80] Gómez-Mejía, L. R. , Haynes, K. T. , Núñez-Nickel, M. , Jacobson, K. J. L. and Moyano-Fuentes, J. (2007) 'Socioemotional Wealth and Business Risks in Family-Controlled Firms: Evidence from Spanish Olive Oil Mills', Administrative Science Quarterly, 52(1), 106 −137.

[81] Gabrenya Jr, W. K. and Hwang, K. -K. (1996) 'Chinese social interaction: Harmony and hierarchy on the good earth' in Bond, M. , ed. , The handbook of Chinese Psychology, Hong Kong: Oxford University Press, 309 −321.

[82] Gallo, M. A. and Sveen, J. (1991) 'Internationalizing the Family Business: Facilitating and Restraining Factors', Family Business Review, 4(2), 181 −190.

[83] Garcia, R. and Calantone, R. (2002) 'A critical look at technological innovation typology and innovativeness terminology: a literature review', Journal of Product Innovation Management, 19(2), 110 −132.

[84] Gargiulo, M. , Ertug, G. and Galunic, C. (2009) 'The Two Faces of Control: Network Closure and Individual Performance among Knowledge Workers', Administrative Science Quarterly, 54(2), 299 −333.

[85] Geiser, C. (2012) Data analysis with Mplus, New York: Guilford Press.

[86] Gelman, A. and Park, D. K. (2009) 'Splitting a predictor at the upper quarter or third and the lower quarter or third', The American Statistician, 63(1).

[87] Goffin, K. and Mitchell, R. (2005) Innovation management: Strategy and implementation using the pentathlon framework, Palgrave Macmillan Houndmills, Basingstoke.

[88] Gopalakrishnan, S. and Damanpour, F. (1997) 'A review of innovation research in economics, sociology and technology management', Omega, 25 (1), 15 −28.

[89] Gouldner, A. W. (1960) 'The Norm of Reciprocity - a Preliminary Statement', American Sociological Review, 25(2), 161 −178.

[90] Granovetter, M. (1973) 'The Strength of Weak Ties', American Journal of Sociology, 78(6), 1360 −1380.

[91] Granovetter, M. (1992) 'Economic Institutions as Social Constructions - a Framework for Analysis', Acta Sociologica, 35(1), 3 −11.

[92] Gu, F. F. , Hung, K. and Tse, D. K. (2008) 'When Does Guanxi Matter? Issues of Capitalization and Its Dark Sides', Journal of Marketing, 72 (4), 12 −28.

[93] Gulati, R. (1995) 'Does Familiarity Breed Trust - the Implications of Repeated Ties for Contractual Choice in Alliances', Academy of Management Journal, 38(1), 85 −112.

[94] Gunday, G. , Ulusoy, G. , Kilic, K. and Alpkan, L. (2011) 'Effects of innovation types on firm performance', International Journal of Production Economics, 133(2), 662 −676.

[95] Gupta, A. K. , Tesluk, P. E. and Taylor, M. S. (2007) 'Innovation at and across Multiple Levels of Analysis', Organization Science, 18(6), 885 −897.

[96] Hair, J. F. , Black, W. C. , Babin, B. J. , Anderson, R. E. and Tatham, R. L. (2006) Multivariate data analysis, Pearson Prentice Hall Upper Saddle River, NJ.

[97] Hair, J. F. , Bush, R. P. and Ortinau, D. J. (2003) Marketing research: Within a changing information environment, Richard D Irwin.

[98] Hall, E. T. (1976) Beyond Culture, New York: Doubleday.

[99] Hansen, M. T. (1999) 'The search-transfer problem: The role of weak ties in sharing knowledge across organization subunits', Administrative Science Quarterly, 44(1), 82 −111.

[100] Hashim, K. F. and Tan, F. B. (2015) 'The mediating role of trust and commitment on members' continuous knowledge sharing intention: A commitment-trust theory perspective', International Journal of Information Management, 35(2), 145 −151.

[101] Hinds, P. , Liu, L. and Lyon, J. (2011) 'Putting the Global in Global Work: An Intercultural Lens on the Practice of Cross-National Collaboration', Academy of Management Annals, 5, 135 −188.

[102] Hitt, M. A. , Beamish, P. W. , Jackson, S. E. and Mathieu, J. E.

(2007) 'Building theoretical and empirical bridges across levels: Multilevel research in management', Academy of Management Journal, 50(6), 1385 – 1399.

[103] Hmieleski, K. M. and Baron, R. A. (2009) 'Entrepreneurs' Optimism And New Venture Performance: A Social Cognitive Perspective', Academy of Management Journal, 52(3), 473 –488.

[104] Hodgkinson, G. P. and Starbuck, W. H. (2008) 'Organizational Decision Making: Mapping Terrains on Different Planets' in Hodgkinson, G. P. and Starbuck, W. H. , eds. , The Oxford handbook of organizational decision making, Oxford: Oxford University Press, 1 –32.

[105] Hofstede, G. (1980) Culture's Consequences: International Difference in Work-Related Values, Beverly Hills, CA: Sage Publications.

[106] Hofstede, G. (1991) Cultures and Organizations: Software of the Mind, London: McGraw-Hill.

[107] Hofstede, G. (2001) Culture's Consequences: Comparing Values, Behaviors, Institutions and Organizations Across Nations, Thousand Oaks, CA: Sage Publications.

[108] Hogg, M. A. and Hains, S. C. (1996) 'Intergroup relations and group solidarity: Effects of group identification and social beliefs on depersonalized attraction', Journal of Personality and Social Psychology, 70(2), 295 – 309.

[109] Holt, D. T. (2012) 'Strategic Decisions Within Family Firms: Understanding the Controlling Family's Receptivity to Internationalization', Entrepreneurship Theory & Practice, 36(6), 1145 –1151.

[110] Hu, L. t. and Bentler, P. M. (1999) 'Cutoff criteria for fit indexes in covariance structure analysis: Conventional criteria versus new alternatives', Structural equation modeling: a multidisciplinary journal, 6(1), 1 –55.

[111] Hwang, K. -k. (1987) 'Face and favor: The Chinese power game', American Journal of Sociology, 944 –974.

[112] Ibarra, H. (1995) 'Race, Opportunity, and Diversity of Social Circles in Managerial Networks', Academy of Management Journal, 38(3), 673 – 703.

[113] Ibarra, H. , Kilduff, M. and Tsai, W. (2005) 'Zooming in and out: Connecting individuals and collectivities at the frontiers of organizational network research', Organization Science, 16(4), 359 –371.

[114] Inkpen, A. C. and Tsang, E. W. K. (2005) 'Social capital, networks, and knowledge transfer', Academy of Management Review, 30(1), 146 – 165.

[115] Jandt, F. E. (2003) An introduction to intercultural communication, San Bernardino: Sage Publications.

[116] Jap, S. D. and Anderson, E. (2003) 'Safeguarding interorganizational performance and continuity under ex post opportunism', Management Science, 49(12), 1684–1701.

[117] Jehn, K. A. and Mannix, E. A. (2001) 'The Dynamic Nature of Conflict: A Longitudinal Study of Intragroup Conflict and Group Performance', Academy of Management Journal, 44(2), 238–251.

[118] Jimenez-Jimenez, D. and Sanz-Valle, R. (2011) 'Innovation, organizational learning, and performance', Journal of Business Research, 64(4), 408–417.

[119] Johnson, J. E., Burlingame, G. M., Olsen, J. A., Davies, D. R. and Gleave, R. L. (2005) 'Group climate, cohesion, alliance, and empathy in group psychotherapy: Multilevel structural equation models', Journal of Counseling Psychology, 52(3), 310.

[120] Jones, T. and Newburn, T. (2002) 'Learning from Uncle Sam? Exploring U. S. Influences on British Crime Control Policy', Governance-an International Journal of Policy Administration and Institutions, 15(1), 97–119.

[121] Kafetzopoulos, D. and Psomas, E. (2015) 'The impact of innovation capability on the performance of manufacturing companies: The Greek case', Journal of Manufacturing Technology Management, 26(1), 104–130.

[122] Kelloway, E. K. (2014) Using Mplus for Structural Equation Modeling: A Researcher's Guide, SAGE Publications.

[123] Kemper, J., Engelen, A. and Brettel, M. (2011) 'How Top Management's Social Capital Fosters the Development of Specialized Marketing Capabilities: A Cross-Cultural Comparison', Journal of International Marketing, 19(3), 87–112.

[124] Kiersch, C. E. (2012) A multi-level examination of authentic leadership and organizational justice in uncertain times, unpublished thesis, Colorado State University.

[125] Kiersch, C. E. and Byrne, Z. S. (2015) 'Is Being Authentic Being Fair? Multilevel Examination of Authentic Leadership, Justice, and Employee Outcomes', Journal of Leadership & Organizational Studies, 22(3), 292–303.

[126] Kim, D., Pan, Y. G. and Park, H. S. (1998) 'High- versus low-context culture: A comparison of Chinese, Korean, and American cultures', Psychology & Marketing, 15(6), 507–521.

[127] Kirkman, B. L. , Chen, G. L. , Farh, J. L. , Chen, Z. X. and Lowe, K. B. (2009) 'Individual Power Distance Orientation and Follower Reactions to Transformational Leaders: A Cross-Level, Cross-Cultural Examination', Academy of Management Journal, 52(4), 744 −764.

[128] Kirkman, B. L. , Lowe, K. B. and Gibson, C. B. (2006) 'A quarter century of Culture's Consequences: a review of empirical research incorporating Hofstede's cultural values framework', Journal of International Business Studies, 37(3), 285 −320.

[129] Kitayama, S. (2002) 'Culture and basic psychological processes - Toward a system view of culture: Comment on Oyserman et al. (2002)', Psychological Bulletin, 128(1), 89 −96.

[130] Klangphahol, K. , Traiwichitkhun, D. and Kanchanawasi, S. (2010) 'Applying multilevel confirmatory factor analysis techniques to perceived homework quality', Research in Higher Education Journal, 6, 1 −10.

[131] Kline, R. B. (2010) Principles and Practice of Structural Equation Modeling New York: Guilford.

[132] Klyver, K. , Lindsay, N. J. , Kassicieh, S. K. S. and Hancock, G. (2017) 'Altruistic investment decision behavior in early-stage ventures', Small Business Economics, 1−18.

[133] Koeszegi, S. , Vetschera, R. and Kersten, G. (2004) 'National cultural differences in the use and perception of internet-based NSS: does high or low context matter?', International Negotiation, 9(1), 79 −109.

[134] Kogut, B. and Zander, U. (1992) 'Knowledge of the Firm, Combinative Capabilities, and the Replication of Technology', Organization Science, 3(3), 383 −397.

[135] Kozlowski, S. W. J. and Klein, K. J. (2000) 'A multilevel approach to theory and research in organizations: Contextual, temporal, and emergent processes', in K Klein & S Kozlowski, Multilevel Theory, Research, & Methods in Organizations: Foundations, Extensions, & New Directions, 3 −90.

[136] Kraatz, M. S. (1998) 'Learning by Association? Interorganizational Networks and Adaptation to Environmental Change', Academy of Management Journal, 41(6), 621 −643.

[137] Krackhardt, D. and Hanson, J. R. (1993) 'Informal networks: the company behind the chart', Harvard Business Review, 71(4), 104.

[138] Kulkarni, S. and Ramamoorthy, N. (2017) 'The Psychological Foundations of Supervisor − Subordinate Information Asymmetry', Organization Studies.

[139] Lüdtke, O. , Trautwein, U. , Kunter, M. and Baumert, J. (2006) 'Reliability and agreement of student ratings of the classroom environment: A reanalysis of TIMSS data', Learning Environments Research, 9(3), 215 − 230.

[140] Lai, H. C. and Gibbons, P. T. (1997) 'Corporate Entrepreneurship: The Roles of Ideology and Social Capital', Group & Organization Management An International Journal, 22(1), 10 −30.

[141] Lam, P. -K. and Chin, K. -S. (2005) 'Identifying and prioritizing critical success factors for conflict management in collaborative new product development', Industrial Marketing Management, 34(8), 761 −772.

[142] Landry, R. , Amara, N. and Lamari, M. (2002) 'Does social capital determine innovation? To what extent?', Technological Forecasting and Social Change, 69(7), 681 −701.

[143] Leana, C. R. and Van Buren, H. J. (1999) 'Organizational social capital and employment practices', Academy of Management Review, 24(3), 538 −555.

[144] Lechner, C. , Frankenberger, K. and Floyd, S. W. (2010) 'Task Contingencies in the Curvilinear Relationships between Intergroup Networks and Initiative Performance', Academy of Management Journal, 53(4), 865 −889.

[145] Lee, H. and Choi, B. (2003) 'Knowledge management enablers, process, and organizational performance: an integrative view and empirical examination', Journal of Management Information Systems, 20(1), 179 − 228.

[146] Leenders, R. T. A. , Van Engelen, J. M. and Kratzer, J. (2003) 'Virtuality, communication, and new product team creativity: a social network perspective', Journal of Engineering and Technology Management, 20 (1), 69 −92.

[147] Leets, L. (2003) 'Disentangling perceptions of subtle racist speech - A cultural perspective', Journal of Language and Social Psychology, 22(2), 145 −168.

[148] Leiva, P. I. , Culbertson, S. S. and Pritchard, R. D. (2011) 'The Empirical Test of an Innovation Implementation Model', The Psychologist-manager Journal, 14(4), 265 −281.

[149] Lesser, E. L. and Storck, J. (2001) 'Communities of practice and organizational performance', Ibm Systems Journal, 40(4), 831 −841.

[150] Leung, K. , Bhagat, R. S. , Buchan, N. R. , Erez, M. and Gibson, C. B. (2005) 'Culture and international business: recent advances and

their implications for future research', Journal of International Business Studies, 36(4), 357 −378.

[151] Levin, D. Z. and Cross, R. (2004) 'The strength of weak ties you can trust: The mediating role of trust in effective knowledge transfer', Management Science, 50(11), 1477 −1490.

[152] Li, B. , Li, C. and Wu, Z. (2017) 'Ownership structure in Japanese banking industry: Evolution and effects', Finance Research Letters.

[153] Li, Y. , Yang, J. , Bai, X. , Che, Y. and Zhan, H. (2012) 'The dark side of entrepreneurs' social capital: From the perspective of relational embeddedness (in Chinese)', China Soft Science, 10, 104 −116.

[154] Li, Y. Q. , Wang, X. H. , Wang, L. L. and Bai, X. (2013) 'How does entrepreneurs' social capital hinder new business development? A relational embeddedness perspective', Journal of Business Research, 66(12).

[155] Lian, H. W. , Ferris, D. L. and Brown, D. J. (2012) 'Does Power Distance Exacerbate or Mitigate the Effects of Abusive Supervision? It Depends on the Outcome', Journal of Applied Psychology, 97(1), 107 − 123.

[156] Liang, X. , Wang, L. and Cui, Z. (2014) 'Chinese Private Firms and Internationalization: Effects of Family Involvement in Management and Family Ownership', Family Business Review, 27(2), 126 −141.

[157] Liden, R. C. (2012) 'Leadership research in Asia: A brief assessment and suggestions for the future', Asia Pacific Journal of Management, 29(2), 205 −212.

[158] Lillis, B. , Szwejczewski, M. and Goffin, K. (2015) 'The development of innovation capability in services: research propositions and management implications', Operations Management Research, 1 −21.

[159] Lin, N. (2001) Social capital: A theory of Social Structure and Action, Cambridge, MA: Cambridge University Press.

[160] Lin, N. , Cook, K. and Burt, R. (2001) Social Capital: Theory and Research, New York: Aldine DE Gruyter.

[161] Liu, S. M. and Liao, J. Q. (2013) 'Transformational Leadership and Speaking Up: Power Distance and Structural Distance as Moderators', Social Behavior and Personality, 41(10), 1747 −1756.

[162] Love, J. H. , Roper, S. and Bryson, J. R. (2011) 'Openness, knowledge, innovation and growth in UK business services', Research Policy, 40(10), 1438 −1452.

[163] Lundvall, B. -Å. (2010) National systems of innovation: Toward a theory of innovation and interactive learning, Anthem Press.

[164] Madlock, P. E. (2012) 'The influence of power distance and communication on Mexican workers', Journal of Business Communication, 49(2), 169 −184.

[165] Magni, M. , Palmi, P. and Salvemini, S. (2017) 'Under pressure! Team innovative climate and individual attitudes in shaping individual improvisation', European Management Journal.

[166] Makela, K. , Kalla, H. K. and Piekkari, R. (2007) 'Interpersonal similarity as a driver of knowledge sharing within multinational corporations', International Business Review, 16(1), 1 −22.

[167] Malhotra, D. (2004) 'Trust and reciprocity decisions: The differing perspectives of trustors and trusted parties', Organizational Behavior and Human Decision Processes, 94(2), 61 −73.

[168] Marsh, H. W. , Ludtke, O. , Nagengast, B. , Trautwein, U. , Morin, A. J. S. , Abduljabbar, A. S. and Koller, O. (2012) 'Classroom Climate and Contextual Effects: Conceptual and Methodological Issues in the Evaluation of Group-Level Effects', Educational Psychologist, 47(2), 106 − 124.

[169] Maurer, I. , Bartsch, V. and Ebers, M. (2011) 'The value of intra-organizational social capital: How it fosters knowledge transfer, innovation performance, and growth', Organization Studies, 32(2), 157 −185.

[170] Maurer, I. and Ebers, M. (2006) 'Dynamics of social capital and their performance implications: Lessons from biotechnology start-ups', Administrative Science Quarterly, 51(2), 262 −292.

[171] McClelland, S. B. (1994) 'Training needs assessment data-gathering methods: Part 1, survey questionnaires', Journal of European Industrial Training, 18(1), 22 −26.

[172] McDermott, C. M. and O'Connor, G. C. (2002) 'Managing radical innovation: an overview of emergent strategy issues', Journal of Product Innovation Management, 19(6), 424 −438.

[173] McFadyen, M. A. and Cannella, A. A. (2004) 'Social capital and knowledge creation: Diminishing returns of the number and strength of exchange relationships', Academy of Management Journal, 47(5), 735 − 746.

[174] McKelvey, M. , Zaring, O. and Ljungberg, D. (2015) 'Creating innovative opportunities through research collaboration: An evolutionary framework and empirical illustration in engineering', Technovation, 39, 26 −36.

[175] McSweeney, B. (2002) 'Hofstede's model of national cultural differences

and their consequences: A triumph of faith - a failure of analysis', Human Relations, 55(1), 89 −118.

[176] Medsker, G. J. , Williams, L. J. and Holahan, P. J. (1994) 'A review of current practices for evaluating causal models in organizational behavior and human resources management research', Journal of Management, 20(2), 439 −464.

[177] Menguc, B. , Auh, S. and Yannopoulos, P. (2014) 'Customer and Supplier Involvement in Design: The Moderating Role of Incremental and Radical Innovation Capability', Journal of Product Innovation Management, 31(2).

[178] Miller, D. and Breton-Miller, I. L. (2006) 'Family Governance and Firm Performance: Agency, Stewardship, and Capabilities ', Family Business Review, 19(1), 73 −87.

[179] Ministry of Science and Technology (2008) 'The administrative Measures for Determination of High and New Tech Enterprises', 172.

[180] Misztal, B. (1996) Trust in Modern Societies, Cambridge: Polity Press.

[181] Mohammed, S. and Dumville, B. C. (2001) 'Team mental models in a team knowledge framework: Expanding theory and measurement across disciplinary boundaries', Journal of Organizational Behavior, 22(2), 89 − 106.

[182] Molina-Morales, F. X. and Martinez-Fernandez, M. T. (2009) 'Too Much Love in the Neighborhood Can Hurt: How an Excess of Intensity and Trust in Relationships May Produce Negative Effects on Firms', Strategic Management Journal, 30(9), 1013 −1023.

[183] Moliterno, T. P. and Mahony, D. M. (2011) 'Network theory of organization: A multilevel approach', Journal of Management, 37(2), 443 − 467.

[184] Monsted, M. (1995) 'Processes and structures of networks: reflections on methodology', Entrepreneurship & Regional Development, 7, 193 −213.

[185] Moran, P. (2005) 'Structural vs. relational embeddedness: Social capital and managerial performance ', Strategic Management Journal, 26 (12), 1129 −1151.

[186] Moreland, R. L. , Levine, J. M. and Turner, M. (2001) 'Socialization in organizations and work groups', Groups at work: Theory and research, 69 −112.

[187] Morgan, R. M. and Hunt, S. D. (1994) 'The commitment-trust theory of relationship marketing', the journal of marketing, 20 −38.

[188] Morgeson, F. P. , Mitchell, T. R. and Liu, D. (2015) 'Event system

theory: An event-oriented approach to the organizational sciences ', Academy of Management Review, 40(4), págs. 515 −537.

[189] Morris, M. W. , Podolny, J. and Sullivan, B. N. (2008) 'Culture and coworker relations: Interpersonal patterns in American, Chinese, German, and Spanish divisions of a global retail bank', Organization Science, 19(4), 517 −532.

[190] Mowery, D. C. and Rosenberg, N. (1999) Paths of innovation: Technological change in 20th-century America, Cambridge University Press.

[191] Muthén, B. O. (1988) Liscomp: Analysisof Linear Structural Equations with a Comprehensive Measurement Model: A Program for Advanced Research, Scientific Software.

[192] Muthén, L. K. and Muthén, B. O. (2012) 'Mplus', The comprehensive modelling program for applied researchers: User's guide, 5.

[193] Nahapiet, J. and Ghoshal, S. (1998) 'Social capital, intellectual capital, and the organizational advantage', Academy of Management Review, 23 (2), 242 −266.

[194] Neuman, W. L. (2006) 'Social research methods: Qualitative and quantitative approaches'.

[195] Ng, K. Y. and Chua, R. Y. J. (2006) 'Do I Contribute More When I Trust More? Differential Effects of Cognition-and Affect-Based Trust ', Management and Organization Review, 2(1), 43 −66.

[196] Nutt, P. C. (2010) 'Comparing the merits of decision making processes' in Nutt, P. C. and Wilson, D. C. , eds. , Handbook of Decision Making, West Sussex, UK: Wiley, 449 −500.

[197] Nutt, P. C. and Wilson, D. C. (2010) 'Crucial trends and issues in strategic decision making' in Nutt, P. C. and Wilson, D. C. , eds. , Handbook of Decision Making, West Sussex, UK: WILEY, 3 −29.

[198] OECD (2005) The measurement of scientific and technological activities Oslo Manual: Guidelines for collecting and interpreting innovation data, Luxembourg: OECD publishing.

[199] OECD (2015) OECD Science, Technology and Industry Scoreboard 2015: Innovation for growth and society, Paris.

[200] Oh, H. , Labianca, G. and Chung, M. H. (2006) 'A multilevel model of group social capital', Academy of Management Review, 31(3), 569 − 582.

[201] Ohly, S. , Sonnentag, S. and Pluntke, F. (2006) 'Routinization, work characteristics and their relationships with creative and proactive behaviors', Journal of Organizational Behavior, 27(3), 257 −279.

[202] Ou, C. X. J. , Davison, R. M. and Wong, L. H. M. (2016) 'Using interactive systems for knowledge sharing: The impact of individual contextual preferences in China', Information & Management, 53(2), 145 – 156.

[203] Pérez-González, F. (2006) 'Inherited Control and Firm Performance', American Economic Review, 96(5), 1559 −1588.

[204] Payne, G. T. , Moore, C. B. , Griffis, S. E. and Autry, C. W. (2011) 'Multilevel Challenges and Opportunities in Social Capital Research', Journal of Management, 37(2), 491−520.

[205] Perlow, L. A. , Gittell, J. H. and Katz, N. (2004) 'Contextualizing patterns of work group interaction: Toward a nested theory of structuration', Organization Science, 15(5), 520 −536.

[206] Perry-Smith, J. E. (2006) 'Social yet creative: The role of social relationships in facilitating individual creativity', Academy of Management Journal, 49(1), 85 −101.

[207] Pervan, S. J. , Bove, L. L. and Johnson, L. W. (2009) 'Reciprocity as a key stabilizing norm of interpersonal marketing relationships: Scale development and validation', Industrial Marketing Management, 38(1), 60 – 70.

[208] Phipps, M. , Ozanne, L. K. , Luchs, M. G. , Subrahmanyan, S. , Kapitan, S. , Catlin, J. R. , Gau, R. , Naylor, R. W. , Rose, R. L. and Simpson, B. (2013) 'Understanding the inherent complexity of sustainable consumption: A social cognitive framework', Journal of Business Research, 66(8), 1227 −1234.

[209] Poder, T. G. (2011) 'What is really social capital? A critical review', The American Sociologist, 42(4), 341 −367.

[210] Porter, M. (1990) The Competitive Advantage of Nations, London: Macmillan.

[211] Portes, A. (1998) 'Social Capital: Its origins and applications in modern sociology', Annual Review of Sociology, 24, 1 −24.

[212] Portes, A. and Sensenbrenner, J. (1993) 'Embeddedness and Immigration - Notes on the Social Determinants of Economic-Action', American Journal of Sociology, 98(6), 1320 −1350.

[213] Powell, W. W. and Smith-Doerr, L. (1994) 'Networks and Economic Life' in Smelser, N. J. and Swedberg, R. , eds. , The Handbook of Economic Sociology, Princeton: Princeton University Press, 368 −402.

[214] Preacher, K. J. , Zyphur, M. J. and Zhang, Z. (2010) 'A general multilevel SEM framework for assessing multilevel mediation ', Psychological

methods, 15(3), 209.

[215] Punch, K. F. (2013) Introduction to social research: Quantitative and qualitative approaches, Sage.

[216] Rass, M. , Dumbach, M. , Danzinger, F. , Bullinger, A. C. and Moeslein, K. M. (2013) 'Open Innovation and Firm Performance: The Mediating Role of Social Capital', Creativity & Innovation Management, 22(2), 177 −194.

[217] Reagans, R. (2005) 'Preferences, identity, and competition: Predicting tie strength from demographic data', Management Science, 51(9), 1374 − 1383.

[218] Reagans, R. and McEvily, B. (2003) 'Network structure and knowledge transfer: The effects of cohesion and range', Administrative Science Quarterly, 48(2), 240 −267.

[219] Reiche, B. S. (2012) 'Knowledge Benefits of Social Capital upon Repatriation: A Longitudinal Study of International Assignees', Journal of Management Studies, 49(6), 1052 −1077.

[220] Richardson, R. M. and Smith, S. W. (2007) 'The influence of high/low-context culture and power distance on choice of communication media: Students' media choice to communicate with professors in Japan and America', International Journal of Intercultural Relations, 31(4), 479 − 501.

[221] Ritala, P. and Hurmelinna-Laukkanen, P. (2013) 'Incremental and Radical Innovation in Coopetition-The Role of Absorptive Capacity and Appropriability', Journal of Product Innovation Management, 30(1), 154 − 169.

[222] Robson, C. (2002) Real world research, Blackwell publishers Oxford.

[223] Rodriguez, N. G. , Perez, M. J. S. and Gutierrez, J. A. T. (2007) 'Interfunctional trust as a determining factor of a new product performance', European Journal of Marketing, 41(5 −6), 678 −702.

[224] Rosenbloom, B. and Larsen, T. (2003) 'Communication in international business-to-business marketing channels - Does culture matter? ', Industrial Marketing Management, 32(4), 309 −315.

[225] Rosso, B. D. (2014) 'Creativity and Constraints: Exploring the Role of Constraints in the Creative Processes of Research and Development Teams', Organization Studies, 35(4), 551 −585.

[226] Ryu, E. (2014) 'Model fit evaluation in multilevel structural equation models', Frontiers in psychology, 5, 81.

[227] Salciuviene, L. , Auruskeviciene, V. and Lydeka, Z. (2005) 'An assess-

ment of various approaches for cross-cultural consumer research', Problems and Perspectives in Management, 3(3), 147 −159.

[228] Savani, K. , Markus, H. R. and Conner, A. L. (2008) 'Let Your Preference Be Your Guide? Preferences and Choices Are More Tightly Linked for North Americans Than for Indians', Journal of Personality and Social Psychology, 95(4), 861 −876.

[229] Schermelleh-Engel, K. , Moosbrugger, H. and Müller, H. (2003) 'Evaluating the fit of structural equation models: Tests of significance and descriptive goodness-of-fit measures', Methods of psychological research online, 8(2), 23 −74.

[230] Schumpeter, J. (1934) The theory of economic development: An inquiry into profits, capital, credit, interest and the business cycle, London: Oxford University Press.

[231] Schumpeter, J. A. (1939) Business cycles: A theoretical historical and statistical analysis and the capitalist process, Cambridge: Cambridge University Press.

[232] Schyns, B. and Sanders, K. (2006) 'Trust, conflict and cooperative behaviour', Personnel Review, 35(5), 508 −518.

[233] Seibert, S. E. , Kraimer, M. L. and Liden, R. C. (2001) 'A social capital theory of career success', Academy of Management Journal, 44(2), 219 −237.

[234] Shane, S. and Stuart, T. (2002) 'Organizational endowments and the performance of university start-ups', Management Science, 48(1), 154 − 170.

[235] Shang, R. A. , Chen, Y. C. and Chen, P. C. (2008) 'Ethical Decisions About Sharing Music Files in the P2P Environment', Journal of Business Ethics, 80(2), 349 −365.

[236] Sheremata, W. A. (2004) 'Competing Through Innovation in Network Markets: Strategies for Challengers', Academy of Management Review, 29(3), 359 −377.

[237] Simons, T. L. and Peterson, R. S. (2000) 'Task conflict and relationship conflict in top management teams: the pivotal role of intragroup trust', Journal of Applied Psychology, 85(1), 102 −11.

[238] Sivakumar, K. and Nakata, C. (2001) 'The stampede toward Hofstede's framework: Avoiding the sample design pit in cross-cultural research', Journal of International Business Studies, 32(3), 555 −574.

[239] Smith, K. G. , Collins, C. J. and Clark, K. D. (2005) 'Existing knowledge, knowledge creation capability, and the rate of new product intro-

duction in high-technology firms', Academy of Management Journal, 48 (2), 346 −357.

[240] Son, S. Y. , Cho, D. H. and Kang, S. W. (2017) 'The impact of close monitoring on creativity and knowledge sharing: The mediating role of leader-member exchange', Creativity & Innovation Management.

[241] Song, F. (2009) 'Intergroup trust and reciprocity in strategic interactions: Effects of group decision-making mechanisms', Organizational Behavior & Human Decision Processes, 108(1), 164 −173.

[242] Song, X. M. and Montoya-weiss, M. M. (1998) 'Critical development activities for really new versus incremental products', Journal of Product Innovation Management, 15(2), 124 −135.

[243] Stapleton, L. M. (2013) 'Multilevel Structural Equation Modeling with Complex Sample Data' in Hancock, G. R. and Mueller, R. O. , eds. , Structural equation modeling: A second course Iap.

[244] Subramaniam, M. and Youndt, M. A. (2005) 'The influence of intellectual capital on the types of innovative capabilities', Academy of Management Journal, 48(3), 450 −463.

[245] Sutcliffe, K. M. and McNamara, G. (2001) 'Controlling decision-making practice in organizations', Organization Science, 12(4), 484 −501.

[246] Swärd, A. (2016) 'Trust, reciprocity, and actions: The development of trust in temporary inter-organizational relations', Organization Studies, 37 (12), 1841 −1860.

[247] Tamjidyamcholo, A. , Bin Baba, M. S. , Tamjid, H. and Gholipour, R. (2013) 'Information security - Professional perceptions of knowledge-sharing intention under self-efficacy, trust, reciprocity, and shared-language', Computers & Education, 68, 223 −232.

[248] Tangpong, C. , Li, J. and Hung, K. T. (2016) 'Dark side of reciprocity norm: Ethical compromise in business exchanges', Industrial Marketing Management, 55, 83 −96.

[249] Taras, V. , Kirkman, B. L. and Steel, P. (2010) 'Examining the impact of Culture's consequences: a three-decade, multilevel, meta-analytic review of Hofstede's cultural value dimensions', Journal of Applied Psychology, 95(3), 405.

[250] TEDA Administrative Commission (2014) 2013 Annual Report of Tianjin Economic-Technological Development Area, Tianjin: Development and Reform Bureau of TEDA.

[251] Temple, B. (1997) 'Watch your tongue: Issues in translation and cross-cultural research', Sociology-the Journal of the British Sociological Associa-

tion, 31(3), 607 −618.

[252] Tsai, W. P. and Ghoshal, S. (1998) 'Social capital and value creation: The role of intrafirm networks', Academy of Management Journal, 41 (4), 464 −476.

[253] Tung, R. L. and Verbeke, A. (2010) 'Beyond Hofstede and GLOBE: Improving the quality of cross-cultural research INTRODUCTION ', Journal of International Business Studies, 41(8), 1259 −1274.

[254] Uhl-Bien, M. and Maslyn, J. M. (2003) 'Reciprocity in Manager-Subordinate Relationships: Components, Configurations, and Outcomes ', Journal of Management, 29(4), 511 −532.

[255] Van de Ven, A. H. , Polley, D. E. , Garud, R. and Venkataraman, S. (1999) 'The innovation journey'.

[256] Van der Panne, G. , van Beers, C. and Kleinknecht, A. (2003) 'Success and Failure of Innovation: A Literature Review', International Journal of Innovation Management, 7(3) .

[257] Varis, M. and Littunen, H. (2010) 'Type of innovation, sources of information and performance in entrepreneurial SMEs', European Journal of Innovation Management, 13(2), 128 −154.

[258] Vidyarthi, P. R. , Anand, S. and Liden, R. C. (2014) 'Do emotionally perceptive leaders motivate higher employee performance? The moderating role of task interdependence and power distance', Leadership Quarterly, 25(2), 232 −244.

[259] Villena, V. H. , Revilla, E. and Choi, T. Y. (2011) 'The dark side of buyer-supplier relationships: A social capital perspective', Journal of Operations Management, 29(6), 561 −576.

[260] Würtz, E. (2005) 'Intercultural Communication on Web sites: A Cross-Cultural Analysis of Web sites from High-Context Cultures and Low-Context Cultures', Journal of Computer-Mediated Communication, 11 (1), 274 −299.

[261] Walsh, J. P. (1995) 'Managerial and organizational cognition: Notes from a trip down memory lane', Organization Science, 6(3), 280 −321.

[262] Wang, J. and Wang, X. (2012) Structural equation modeling: Applications using Mplus, John Wiley & Sons.

[263] Warner-Søderholm, G. (2013) 'Beyond a Literature Review of Hall's Context Dimension: Scale Development, Validation & Empirical Findings within a Norwegian Study', International Journal of Business and Management, 8(10), 27 −40.

[264] Wasko, M. M. and Faraj, S. (2005) 'Why should I share? Examining

social capital and knowledge contribution in electronic networks of practice',
Mis Quarterly, 29(1), 35 −57.

[265] Weber, E. U. , Ames, D. R. and Blais, A. (2005) " How Do I Choose
Thee? Let me Count the Ways': A Textual Analysis of Similarities and
Differences in Modes of Decision-making in China and the United States',
Management and Organization Review, 1(1), 87 −118.

[266] Weber, E. U. , Ames, D. R. and Blais, A. R. (2005) " How Do I
Choose Thee? Let me Count the Ways': A Textual Analysis of Similarities
and Differences in Modes of Decision-making in China and the United
States', Social Science Electronic Publishing, 1(1), 87 −118.

[267] Webster, C. and White, A. (2010) 'Exploring the national and organizational culture mix in service firms', Journal of the Academy of Marketing
Science, 38(6), 691 −703.

[268] Wicker, A. W. (1979) The Social Psychology of Organizing, 2d ed. by
Karl E. Weick, McGraw-Hill, Inc.

[269] Williams, C. (2015) Effective management, Cengage Learning.

[270] Wong, K. S. S. (2013) 'The role of management involvement in innovation', Management Decision, 51(4), 709 −729.

[271] Wu, P. C. and Chaturvedi, S. (2009) 'The Role of Procedural Justice
and Power Distance in the Relationship Between High Performance Work
Systems and Employee Attitudes: A Multilevel Perspective', Journal of
Management Official Journal of the Southern Management Association, 35
(5), 1228 −1247.

[272] Wu, W. P. (2008) 'Dimensions of social capital and firm competitiveness
improvement: The mediating role of information sharing', Journal of
Management Studies, 45(1), 122 −146.

[273] Xiao, Z. and Su, S. K. (2004) 'Keeping others in mind: A very social
cognition of Asian managers ' in Leung, K. and White, S. , eds. , Handbook of Asian Management, Hingham: Kluwer Academic Publishers, 315 −
347.

[274] Xiao, Z. X. and Tsui, A. S. (2007) 'When brokers may not work: The
cultural contingency of social capital in Chinese high-tech firms', Administrative Science Quarterly, 52(1), 1 −31.

[275] Yang, J. , Mossholder, K. W. and Peng, T. K. (2007) 'Procedural justice climate and group power distance: an examination of cross-level interaction effects', Journal of Applied Psychology, 92(3), 681.

[276] Yates, J. F. and Oliveira, S. D. (2016) 'Culture and decision making',
Organizational Behavior & Human Decision Processes, 136, 106 −118.

[277] Yli-Renko, H. , Autio, E. and Sapienza, H. J. (2001) 'Social capital, knowledge acquisition, and knowledge exploitation in young technology-based firms', Strategic Management Journal, 22(6-7), 587 −613.

[278] Yu, S. H. (2013) 'Social capital, absorptive capability, and firm innovation', Technological Forecasting and Social Change, 80(7), 1261−1270.

[279] Yu, Y. , Hao, J. X. , Dong, X. Y. and Khalifa, M. (2013) 'A multi-level model for effects of social capital and knowledge sharing in knowledge-intensive work teams', International Journal of Information Management.

[280] Yuan, F. and Woodman, R. W. (2010) 'Innovative behavior in the workplace: The role of performance and image outcome expectations', Academy of Management Journal, 53(2), 323 −342.

[281] Zahra, S. A. and Garvis, D. M. (2000) 'International corporate entrepreneurship and firm performance : The moderating effect of international environmental hostility', Journal of Business Venturing, 15(5), 469 −492.

[282] Zhang, Z. , Zhang, X. and Cui, R. (2013) 'Research on the effects of WTO accession on China's economic growth: Path analysis and empirical study', Journal of Chinese Economic and Foreign Trade Studies, 6(2), 70 −84.

[283] Zheng, W. (2010) 'A Social Capital Perspective of Innovation from Individuals to Nations: Where is Empirical Literature Directing Us?', International Journal of Management Reviews, 12(2), 151 −183.

[284] Zhou, K. Z. , Zhang, Q. Y. , Sheng, S. B. , Xie, E. and Bao, Y. Q. (2014) 'Are relational ties always good for knowledge acquisition? Buyer-supplier exchanges in China', Journal of Operations Management, 32(3), 88 −98.

Appendices

Appendix 1   Survey

Survey A

Dear managers,

The purpose of my research is to explore the relationship between social capital and innovation. Your participation in the study will involve completing a survey about your firm's innovation performance. This is because as a manager, you are the one most able to determine and influence your firm's innovation activities.

Your participation in this survey is purely voluntary. You have the right to refuse to answer any or all of the questions, or to withdraw from participating at any time.

Please be assured that information you provide in this survey will be kept confidential and the result of the survey will only be used for academic purpose. Also, the survey is anonymous and does not involve identifying you or your firm specifically. If you have any questions about this study or would like more information, please feel free to contact me at the address below.

Thank you in advance for your co-operation in making my research possible.

Your sincerely,
Zhan Wang

The following questions ask about your firm's innovation performance during the last three years

1. How many new products has your firm introduced?

Period	New product	Quantity
2011	New to the world	
	New to the firm	
	Major change	
present	Minor change	

2. How many new methods of product manufacturing has your firm introduced?

Period	Process innovation	Quantity
2011	New or significant improved methods of manufacturing or producing goods	
	New or significantly improved logistics for your inputs or goods	
present	New or significantly improved supporting activities for process, such as maintenance systems, operation for purchasing, accounting or computing	

3. How many new marketing methods have been introduced in your firm?

Period	Marketing innovation	Quantity
2011	New or significant changes to the aesthetic design or packaging of a good	
	New media or techniques for product promotion	
	New methods for sales channels	
present	New methods of pricing goods	

4. How many new systems or programs have been introduced in your firm?

Period	Organizational innovation	Quantity
2011	New systems of quality management	
	New systems of supply chain management	
	New systems of knowledge management	
	New methods of organizing external relations with other firms or public institutions such as partnerships, government or outsourcing	
present	New education or training system	
	New methods of organizing work responsibilities	

Survey B

Dear Participant,

I am Zhan Wang. The purpose of my research is to explore the relationship between social capital and innovation. Your participation in the study will involve completing a survey.

There are three sections in the survey:

• Section A asks about some brief personal information, which is anticipated to take 3—5 minutes to complete.

• Section B asks you to identify 2 people which usually work with you currently (in the last one year period), and answer questions about how you interact with each of them. This section will take about 10 minutes to complete.

• Section C asks about your attitudes, which will take about 5 minutes to complete.

Your participation in this survey is purely voluntary. You have the right to refuse to answer any or all of the questions, or to withdraw from participating at any time.

Please be assured that information you provide in this survey will be kept confidential. Also, the survey is anonymous and the result of survey will only be used for academic purposes.

If you have any questions about this study or would like more information, please feel free to contact me at the address below.

Thank you in advance for your co-operation in making my research possible.

Your sincerely,
Zhan Wang

Section A

This section seeks general information about you.

1. What is your age?

○ 18—22   ○ 23—28   ○ 29—35   ○ 36—42
○ 43—50   ○ 50—60   ○ over 60

2. Please indicate your highest level of education achievement.

○ High school   ○ Bachelor   ○ Master   ○ PhD

3. Have you ever worked/studied abroad for more than one year?

○ Yes   ○ No

4. If yes, please indicate the country ____, and how long were you there?

○ 12—23 months   ○ 24—35 months

○ 36—47 months   ○ more than 48 months

Section B

If you look back over the last one year period, who are the people with whom you usually work? Please identify two people who should be (1) a direct supervisor and (2) a colleague you usually work with. It is not necessary to provide their real names. Instead, use the "S" for the direct supervisor and "C" for your colleague. Now considering these two people, please respond regarding the relationship you have with each person.

1. When communicating with each other, C and I can use understandable language.

○ Strongly disagree ○ Disagree ○ Somewhat disagree ○ Undecided
○ Somewhat agree ○ Agree ○ Strongly agree

2. When communicating with each other, S and I can use understandable language.

○ Strongly disagree ○ Disagree ○ Somewhat disagree ○ Undecided
○ Somewhat agree ○ Agree ○ Strongly agree

3. C and I have same interests.

○ Strongly disagree ○ Disagree ○ Somewhat disagree ○ Undecided
○ Somewhat agree ○ Agree ○ Strongly agree

4. S and I have same interest.

○ Strongly disagree ○ Disagree ○ Somewhat disagree ○ Undecided
○ Somewhat agree ○ Agree ○ Strongly agree

5. C and I could not take advantage of each other even if the opportunity occurs.

○ Strongly disagree ○ Disagree ○ Somewhat disagree ○ Undecided
○ Somewhat agree ○ Agree ○ Strongly agree

6. S and I could not take advantage of each other even if the opportunity occurs.

○ Strongly disagree ○ Disagree ○ Somewhat disagree ○ Undecided
○ Somewhat agree ○ Agree ○ Strongly agree

7. I need to concern about C's benefits when making decisions related to work issues.

○ Strongly disagree ○ Disagree ○ Somewhat disagree ○ Undecided

○ Somewhat agree ○ Agree ○ Strongly agree

8. I need to concern about C's benefit when making decisions related to work issues.

○ Strongly disagree ○ Disagree ○ Somewhat disagree ○ Undecided
○ Somewhat agree ○ Agree ○ Strongly agree

9. C and I can keep the promises we make to one another.

○ Strongly disagree ○ Disagree ○ Somewhat disagree ○ Undecided
○ Somewhat agree ○ Agree ○ Strongly agree

10. S and I can keep the promises we make to one another.

○ Strongly disagree ○ Disagree ○ Somewhat disagree ○ Undecided
○ Somewhat agree ○ Agree ○ Strongly agree

11. I know that C would help me, so it is only fair to help C.

○ Strongly disagree ○ Disagree ○ Somewhat disagree ○ Undecided
○ Somewhat agree ○ Agree ○ Strongly agree

12. I know that S would help me, so it is only fair to help S.

○ Strongly disagree ○ Disagree ○ Somewhat disagree ○ Undecided
○ Somewhat agree ○ Agree ○ Strongly agree

13. C and I prefer to use the same mean to communicate with each other (e. g. , face to face, text, Email etc.).

○ Strongly disagree ○ Disagree ○ Somewhat disagree ○ Undecided
○ Somewhat agree ○ Agree ○ Strongly agree

14. S and I prefer to use the same mean to communicate with each other (e. g. , face to face, text, Email etc.).

○ Strongly disagree ○ Disagree ○ Somewhat disagree ○ Undecided
○ Somewhat agree ○ Agree ○ Strongly agree

15. I have to give up my initial decisions due to "renqing" issues with C.

○ Strongly disagree ○ Disagree ○ Somewhat disagree ○ Undecided
○ Somewhat agree ○ Agree ○ Strongly agree

16. I have to give up my initial decisions due to "renqing" issues with S.

○ Strongly disagree ○ Disagree ○ Somewhat disagree ○ Undecided
○ Somewhat agree ○ Agree ○ Strongly agree

17. Neither C and I knowingly do anything to disrupt the communication.

○ Strongly disagree ○ Disagree ○ Somewhat disagree ○ Undecided
○ Somewhat agree ○ Agree ○ Strongly agree

18. Neither S and I knowingly do anything to disrupt the communication.

○ Strongly disagree ○ Disagree ○ Somewhat disagree ○ Undecided
○ Somewhat agree ○ Agree ○ Strongly agree

19. When working together, C and I share similar goals and principles re-

garding work-related problems.

○ Strongly disagree ○ Disagree ○ Somewhat disagree ○ Undecided
○ Somewhat agree ○ Agree ○ Strongly agree

20. When working together, S and I share similar goals and principles regarding work-related problems.

○ Strongly disagree ○ Disagree ○ Somewhat disagree ○ Undecided
○ Somewhat agree ○ Agree ○ Strongly agree

21. I trust that C would help me if I were in a similar situation.

○ Strongly disagree ○ Disagree ○ Somewhat disagree ○ Undecided
○ Somewhat agree ○ Agree ○ Strongly agree

22. I trust that S would help me if I were in a similar situation.

○ Strongly disagree ○ Disagree ○ Somewhat disagree ○ Undecided
○ Somewhat agree ○ Agree ○ Strongly agree

23. It is imperative to consider C's concern when making decisions.

○ Strongly disagree ○ Disagree ○ Somewhat disagree ○ Undecided
○ Somewhat agree ○ Agree ○ Strongly agree

24. It is imperative to consider S's concern when making decisions.

○ Strongly disagree ○ Disagree ○ Somewhat disagree ○ Undecided
○ Somewhat agree ○ Agree ○ Strongly agree

25. When working together, C and I share similar values about which behaviour is appropriate or right.

○ Strongly disagree ○ Disagree ○ Somewhat disagree ○ Undecided
○ Somewhat agree ○ Agree ○ Strongly agree

26. When working together, S and I share similar values about which behaviour is appropriate or right.

○ Strongly disagree ○ Disagree ○ Somewhat disagree ○ Undecided
○ Somewhat agree ○ Agree ○ Strongly agree

27. It is impossible to make decisions completely according to my own preferences because I have to consider C.

○ Strongly disagree ○ Disagree ○ Somewhat disagree ○ Undecided
○ Somewhat agree ○ Agree ○ Strongly agree

28. It is impossible to make decisions completely according to my own preferences because I have to consider S.

○ Strongly disagree ○ Disagree ○ Somewhat disagree ○ Undecided
○ Somewhat agree ○ Agree ○ Strongly agree

29. Both C and I behave in a consistent manner.

○ Strongly disagree ○ Disagree ○ Somewhat disagree ○ Undecided
○ Somewhat agree ○ Agree ○ Strongly agree

30. Both S and I behave in a consistent manner.
○ Strongly disagree ○ Disagree ○ Somewhat disagree ○ Undecided
○ Somewhat agree ○ Agree ○ Strongly agree

31. Both C and I are truthful in dealing with one another.
○ Strongly disagree ○ Disagree ○ Somewhat disagree ○ Undecided
○ Somewhat agree ○ Agree ○ Strongly agree

32. Both S and I are truthful in dealing with one another.
○ Strongly disagree ○ Disagree ○ Somewhat disagree ○ Undecided
○ Somewhat agree ○ Agree ○ Strongly agree

33. The relationship with C constrains my freedom in making decisions related to work.
○ Strongly disagree ○ Disagree ○ Somewhat disagree ○ Undecided
○ Somewhat agree ○ Agree ○ Strongly agree

34. The relationship with S constraints my freedom in making decisions related to work.
○ Strongly disagree ○ Disagree ○ Somewhat disagree ○ Undecided
○ Somewhat agree ○ Agree ○ Strongly agree

35. How often do you communicate with C?
○ Daily ○ Twice a week ○ Once a week ○ Twice a month
○ Once a month ○ Once every two months
○ Once every 3 months or less or never

36. How often do you communicate with S?
○ Daily ○ Twice a week ○ Once a week ○ Twice a month
○ Once a month ○ Once every two months
○ Once every 3 months or less or never

37. How close is your working relationship with C?
○ Very distance ○ Distance ○ Somewhat distance ○ Undecided
○ Somewhat close ○ Close ○ Very close

38. How close is your working relationship with S?
○ Very distance ○ Distance ○ Somewhat distance ○ Undecided
○ Somewhat close ○ Close ○ Very close

Section C

This section asks you about your attitudes about…

1. In most situations, superiors should make decisions without consulting their subordinates.
○ Strongly disagree ○ Disagree ○ Somewhat disagree ○ Undecided

○ Somewhat agree ○ Agree ○ Strongly agree

2. Employees should not express disagreements with their superiors.

○ Strongly disagree ○ Disagree ○ Somewhat disagree ○ Undecided

○ Somewhat agree ○ Agree ○ Strongly agree

3. Honesty is valued in meetings and discussions.

○ Strongly disagree ○ Disagree ○ Somewhat disagree ○ Undecided

○ Somewhat agree ○ Agree ○ Strongly agree

4. In work-related matters, superiors have a right to expect obedience from their subordinates.

○ Strongly disagree ○ Disagree ○ Somewhat disagree ○ Undecided

○ Somewhat agree ○ Agree ○ Strongly agree

5. A company's rules should not be broken—not even when the employee thinks it is in the company's best interest.

○ Strongly disagree ○ Disagree ○ Somewhat disagree ○ Undecided

○ Somewhat agree ○ Agree ○ Strongly agree

6. I usually try to avoid showing disagreement openly in a discussion because we prefer to maintain a sense of harmony in meeting.

○ Strongly disagree ○ Disagree ○ Somewhat disagree ○ Undecided

○ Somewhat agree ○ Agree ○ Strongly agree

7. Employees who often question authority sometimes keep their superiors from being effective.

○ Strongly disagree ○ Disagree ○ Somewhat disagree ○ Undecided

○ Somewhat agree ○ Agree ○ Strongly agree

8. I like to "say it as it is".

○ Strongly disagree ○ Disagree ○ Somewhat disagree ○ Undecided

○ Somewhat agree ○ Agree ○ Strongly agree

9. Once a superior makes a decision, subordinates should not question it.

○ Strongly disagree ○ Disagree ○ Somewhat disagree ○ Undecided

○ Somewhat agree ○ Agree ○ Strongly agree

10. I believe that maintaining harmony and a positive tone in a meeting is more important than speaking honestly.

○ Strongly disagree ○ Disagree ○ Somewhat disagree ○ Undecided

○ Somewhat agree ○ Agree ○ Strongly agree

11. Superiors should be able to make the right decisions without consulting with others.

○ Strongly disagree ○ Disagree ○ Somewhat disagree ○ Undecided

○ Somewhat agree ○ Agree ○ Strongly agree

12. Superiors who let their subordinates participate in decisions may lose

power.

○ Strongly disagree ○ Disagree ○ Somewhat disagree ○ Undecided
○ Somewhat agree ○ Agree ○ Strongly agree

Thank you very much for completing this survey!

Appendix 2 Descriptive statistics of every survey item

Table A1   Descriptive statistics

	Min	Max	Mean	Std. Deviation	Skewness		Kurtosis	
	Statistic	Statistic	Statistic	Statistic	Statistic	Std. Error	Statistic	Std. Error
TSC1	1	7	4.93	1.665	-.592	.065	-.501	.131
TSC2	1	7	4.72	1.789	-.419	.065	-.836	.131
TSS1	1	7	4.88	1.642	-.612	.065	-.341	.131
TSS2	1	7	4.62	1.776	-.390	.065	-.829	.131
SCC1	1	7	5.48	1.438	-1.375	.065	1.864	.131
SCC2	1	7	5.22	1.509	-1.030	.065	.708	.131
SCC3	1	7	4.47	1.573	-.150	.065	-.414	.131
SCC4	1	7	4.80	1.421	-.479	.065	-.068	.131
SCC5	1	7	4.85	1.547	-.494	.065	-.320	.131
SCS1	1	7	5.44	1.431	-1.374	.065	1.830	.131
SCS2	1	7	4.53	1.571	-.414	.065	.260	.131
SCS3	1	7	4.93	1.511	-.652	.065	.090	.131
SCS4	1	7	4.82	1.609	-.531	.065	-.352	.131
SCS5	1	7	4.87	1.556	-.555	.065	-.228	.131
NRC1	1	7	4.80	1.447	-.393	.065	-.083	.131
NRC2	1	7	4.77	1.482	-.498	.065	.075	.131
NRS1	1	7	4.70	1.503	-.433	.065	-.098	.131
NRS2	1	7	4.74	1.495	-.430	.065	-.132	.131
TRC1	1	7	4.56	1.657	-.258	.065	-.727	.131
TRC2	1	7	4.76	1.634	-.413	.065	-.620	.131
TRC3	1	7	4.84	1.635	-.436	.065	-.696	.131
TRC4	1	7	4.62	1.710	-.287	.065	-.887	.131
TRC5	1	7	4.55	1.718	-.253	.065	-.923	.131

continued

	Min	Max	Mean	Std. Deviation	Skewness		Kurtosis	
	Statistic	Statistic	Statistic	Statistic	Statistic	Std. Error	Statistic	Std. Error
TRS1	1	7	4. 57	1. 675	−. 225	. 065	−. 839	. 131
TRS2	1	7	4. 67	1. 648	−. 347	. 065	−. 712	. 131
TRS3	1	7	4. 65	1. 696	−. 255	. 065	−. 936	. 131
TRS4	1	7	4. 68	1. 660	−. 323	. 065	−. 774	. 131
TRS5	1	7	4. 61	1. 680	−. 269	. 065	−. 842	. 131
SDC1	1	7	4. 46	1. 789	−. 232	. 065	−. 975	. 131
SDC2	1	7	4. 33	1. 796	−. 117	. 065	-1. 016	. 131
SDC3	1	7	4. 39	1. 770	−. 143	. 065	−. 949	. 131
SDC4	1	7	4. 50	1. 755	−. 248	. 065	−. 892	. 131
SDC5	1	7	4. 73	1. 699	−. 461	. 065	−. 607	. 131
SDS1	1	7	4. 75	1. 750	−. 411	. 065	−. 699	. 131
SDS2	1	7	4. 63	1. 775	−. 370	. 065	−. 818	. 131
SDS3	1	7	4. 67	1. 774	−. 373	. 065	−. 805	. 131
SDS4	1	7	4. 74	1. 732	−. 448	. 065	−. 649	. 131
SDS5	1	7	4. 96	1. 720	−. 639	. 065	−. 330	. 131
PRODI	3	51	17. 09	9. 621	. 546	. 065	−. 096	. 131
PROCI	3	50	17. 03	11. 441	1. 026	. 065	. 414	. 131
MARKI	3	36	14. 61	8. 021	. 746	. 065	−. 142	. 131
ORGAI	4	56	21. 90	11. 328	. 613	. 065	−. 211	. 131
PD1	1	7	3. 94	1. 662	. 137	. 065	−. 713	. 131
PD2	1	7	4. 92	1. 499	−. 604	. 065	−. 029	. 131
PD3	1	7	4. 79	1. 575	−. 583	. 065	−. 276	. 131
PD4	1	7	4. 01	1. 693	. 169	. 065	−. 775	. 131
PD5	1	7	4. 09	1. 613	. 119	. 065	−. 720	. 131
PD6	1	7	4. 93	1. 523	−. 768	. 065	. 199	. 131
PD7	1	7	4. 02	1. 668	. 171	. 065	−. 741	. 131
PD8	1	7	5. 57	1. 472	-1. 401	. 065	1. 712	. 131
HLC1	1	7	3. 43	1. 666	. 825	. 065	−. 113	. 131
HLC2	1	7	4. 87	1. 595	−. 455	. 065	−. 543	. 131
HLC3	1	7	3. 53	1. 645	. 764	. 065	−. 122	. 131
HLC4	1	7	4. 84	1. 611	−. 459	. 065	−. 570	. 131

This book is the result of a co-publication agreement between China Financial and Economic Publishing House (China) and Paths International Ltd (UK).

Title: Social Capital's Impact on Innovation: Bright Side, Dark Side or Both?
Author: Wang Zhan
ISBN: 978-1-84464-732-3
Ebook ISBN: 978-1-84464-733-0

Paths International Ltd

Published in the United Kingdom
www.pathsinternational.com

9 781844 647323